T0065161

OTHER BOOKS AUTHORED BY DR OLERIBE INCLUDE;

- Celebrating Marital Success
- Repositioning for Marital Success
- Scaling New Heights
- Making Maximum Impact In Life
- Transforming Ideas, Seed for Entrepreneurship and Greatness
- Deliberate Proactive Leadership
- The Concept of Child Abuja
- Fundamentals of Child Rights
- ADJS at 40: Celebrating Excellence, Consolidating the Vision (Editor)

REBUILDING NIGERIA

Solutions

that

Make

Sense.

OBINNA OSITADIMMA OLERIBE

authorHOUSE

AuthorHouse™
1663 Liberty Drive
Bloomington, IN 47403
www.authorhouse.com
Phone: 833-262-8899

Published by AuthorHouse 07/30/2020

ISBN: 978-1-7283-6806-1 (sc)
ISBN: 978-1-7283-6895-5 (e)

Library of Congress Control Number: 2020914372

Dedicated

To Ogechi, my twin sister and all Nigerians who lost their lives to the present chaos called Nigeria

Contents

Acknowledgements ix

Chapter 1:   The Problems and
             Challenges of Nigeria..................... 1
Chapter 2:   The Perpetuating Factors.............. 21
Chapter 3:   The Effects and Impacts 38
Chapter 4:   The Strategies, Solutions and
             Systems 57
Chapter 5:   Change Begins with Me
             (#CBWM) 95
Chapter 6:   Building a Nation that Makes
             Sense: The Need for a
             Unique Identity for Each
             Nigerian.....................................109
Chapter 7:   Heralding United Nations of
             Nigeria (UNON)............................117
Chapter 8:   The COVID-19:
             Comprehensive Containment
             Strategy...................................... 124

Appendix 1... 139
Appendix 2... 143
Appendix 3...147
Appendix 4...151
Appendix 5... 157

Acknowledgements

I want to thank all those who have stood the test of time in rebuilding Nigeria from the ashes, especially all who responded to my survey for this study. Your honesty was very encouraging and revealed your desire for a better Nigeria.

I thank my father, Mr Nwadike Wilfred Oleribe (Willie) who exemplified a good and dedicated Nigerian, and taught me the first principles in nationalism and humanity. I am grateful to my wife, Princess Osita Oleribe for all her support in my literary works, and my editors, Mr Chisom Anukam, Madeshola Adeduro, and Sr. Gladys Dimaku, MMM for their excellent proof reading. Mr Anndy Omoluabi gave tremendous IT support.

I thank you, in advance, for buying/receiving, reading, meditating and working to make happen every single sensible strategy, solution and option in this book.

I welcome you to a new and properly rebranded Nigeria.

Obinna O Oleribe

+234 803 547 3223
+1 541 892 2896
droleribe@yahoo.com
obinna.oleribe@expertmanagers.org

Pulse and Reflect:
Nigeria was Great, and Shall be Great AGAIN

Let me begin this book in a positive note. Nigeria shall be great again! I have lived in this country long enough to know that Nigeria is one of the greatest nations of the world. It is also the most blessed nation with excellent weather, wonderful people, great landscape, sufficient natural resources and amazing sociocultural practices.

Years ago, I travelled out to work in another African country. But despite the excellent pay and wonderful benefits, I had to return to Nigeria after a year to begin afresh – because I strongly missed my country.

People complain about the absence of electric power, corruption at high and low places, poor infrastructures, and even unskilled leadership at all levels. These are true. But what we fail to tell the world about our good country are the wonderful things we have as a nation - the people, the food, the game reserves, and the weather.

Am I saying that there are no bad things in Nigeria? No. Like in any other country, there are so many bad things happening in this Nigeria – Boko Haram in the north, kidnapping in the south, abuse of office in Abuja, the Federal Capital Territory, and corruption by the high and mighty as well as by the drivers and messengers, and several others. The social vices and economic crimes in any country are peculiar to that country as a result of their political and socio-economic exposure and experiences. However, there are more good things happening in this country than the bad things. I believe that the time has come for us to refocus and begin to tell the world the good things in our nation, play positive roles to make the country a better place, and work tirelessly to ensure that we leave a greater country for our children than the one our fathers left for us.

For instance, I brought to completion the house my father left behind. Beyond the buildings made of bricks and walls, every seed of goodness left behind by our forefathers are to be magnified by us to produce a giant tree of which the next generation can further work upon. With this, we wouldn't be found playing the blame game.

We have over the years blamed everything and everybody for the present state of the nation. Never have we blamed ourselves. It is time to take full responsibility for our nation and work to see it better. Nigeria can and should be great again! I believe this and I want you to believe it with me. We can make Nigeria great again. We can change the face of Nigeria and give her a new brand. I am not speaking about lying to ourselves in the name of rebranding Nigeria, but doing the right things to rebrand the country.

This informed my decision to call for a **MINUTE** prayer for Nigeria every first day of a new month by **9.00 pm**. This we began in the month of April 2016. The response was amazing. A friend and his family visited me on April 1st and stayed till 9.00 PM. We had an extended family prayer for Nigeria with the visiting family. What an awesome experience. We all enjoyed it, and yes, my family and friends were glad to be part of this process. I look forward to every 1st when again we will pray for Nigeria. Someone may be saying that we have prayed enough. That prayer is not what Nigeria needs. This statement is far from the truth because you can never pray enough. We cannot claim to have prayed enough until we have our desired nation. Therefore, join us next 1st of the month and together we will move Nigeria forward.

What is unique about this prayer group? We not only pray for Nigeria, but also get involved in social change activities every month. Many members have executed several excellent social change activities. Some cleaned the gutters, some paid peoples' fees, some helped the widows and orphans, some visited the prison, and some attended multiracial marriages and made a difference. Also, some visited the poor and supported them financially, some even counselled people on various issues of life, some gave money to non-governmental organizations, etc. As the reports keep coming, it amazes me how simple steps can trigger such a global social change movement.

Will you join us? Pray for Nigeria every 1st day of the month by **9.00 PM**. This can be as short as just for a Minute. Do something good to someone every **15th day** of the month. This should be planned and implemented. To change Nigeria and see her great again, we all MUST do something positive. Let us save our energy from complaining about what is not working and invest our energy into making things work. Let us desist from the blame game and subscribe to the burden sharing game – where we bear the burden of Nigeria for Nigeria and the rest of the world.

If you truly care for Nigeria, now is the time to play a crucial role to revitalize the country, rebuild her systems and institutionalize good practices. It is time to live by example and be the change we all want to see. It is time to stand out from the crowd and take a place in the hall of fame of good and proud Nigerians. Will you join us to make history? Will you join us to change this country positively? Now is the time for the change you have long waited to see. Let us together make it happen.

Nigeria shall be great again. My Vision for Nigeria is to see Nigeria become a free first world nation. We can make a difference towards the realization of an advanced African Continent, work with likeminded individuals to leave a legacy by empowering Africans to succeed through mentorship, trainings and psychological reprogramming. This is the essence of this book. Together, we can make Nigeria great again.

Rebuilding Nigeria:
The Genesis

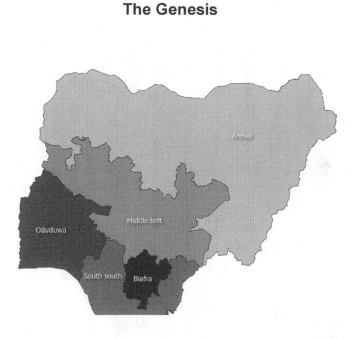

I am a Nigerian of the Igbo extraction. I was born just before the end of the civil war to Mr Nwadike Wilfred Oleribe and Mrs Mercy Ure Oleribe who were teachers before and after the Nigeria civil war. My parents actually considered aborting me as they did not have what it would require to raise us. This is because the war saw their female daughters suffering from Kwashiorkor and Marasmus, and they did not want to bring me into the world to suffer. My twin sister, Ogechi, died a few months after birth.

I have lived most of my life in Nigeria – born in the South East, Schooled in the South-South, served the mandatory one year National Youth Service Corps (NYSC) in the South-West and have worked for 20 years plus in the North Central Nigeria. I have also supported public health activities, carried out researches and executed projects in all geopolitical parts of Nigeria. In addition, I have travelled to over 15 nations of the world and seen how things work in these places.

I have two bachelor's degrees, three masters, a doctorate and five fellowships. I was a multiple award winner at secondary, tertiary and post graduate levels of my training. I have worked for public, private and now self-established sectors of the national economy. I have seen it all!

In April 2016, I began a social change movement for a better Nigeria; and added the Nigeria must Be Better (NMBB) Campaign which necessitated monthly prayers for the nation on the first of every month. I later convened the first Nigerian Solution Summit in Abuja to find answers to national challenges in 2018. Since then, we have been taking steps to see a new and better Nigeria.

But Nigeria is still not delivered. So, the need to do something extra. To this end, I developed and circulated a simple questionnaire using Monkey Survey to pick the minds of excellent Nigerians on some key topical issues concerning the nation.

Apart from demographics (region, age, gender, educational qualification and religion), I asked just five simple questions:

1) What do you think are the three key problems or challenges facing Nigeria as a nation?
2) What do you think are the three major root cause(s) of these problems?
3) What do you think are the three main perpetuating factors sustaining these problems and challenges?
4) What do you think are the three main possible solutions for Nigeria out of these problems?
5) Which problem should Nigerian Government focus on as a priority?

In sending out the Survey, I added: *Do you desire a new Nigeria? Do you have solutions that make sense to our National problems? Can you spare 10 minutes to share these solutions? Please click and respond to this short questionnaire. Thank you Dr. Obinna Oleribe*

This book is a summary of my beliefs and findings from this survey. Is there an element of bias –as I reached out primarily to my friends, contacts and their contacts.

Monkey Survey was shared on Monday, March 2, 2020 and closed on March 4, 2020 after over a 100 people completed the exercise. At the end of the exercise, 103 persons completed the questionnaire.

Three questionnaires were not analysed as they were not properly completed. First 100 questionnaires were analysed using the Monkey Survey analysis Tools and MS Excel.

This book Rebuilding Nigeria: Solutions that Make Sense will provide a template for a New Nigeria. My parents are no longer with us, and will not see this new Nigeria, but I want my children to see it. We have a responsibility to make this nation a better place for them and their children's children.

I believe that together, we can build and see a better Nigeria in our lifetimes.

God bless you.

Why This Book?

Nigeria ought to be the giant of Africa, but a lot of waters have passed under the bridge. Today, there is the need to take hard decisions, make hard choices and pay the price for a new Nigeria. I have seen Nigeria deteriorate from bad to worse. I have seen the good, the bad and the ugly. Having lived most of my life here, and in all parts of Nigeria North, South, East and West; I feel committed to be part of the solution and not the problem. I am from the East, schooled in South-South, did National Youth Service and worked briefly in South West, and have worked for over 20 years now in North Central. I have also travelled extensively across North East and North West where I helped establish programs for The President's Emergency Plan for Aids Relief (PEPFAR) and Global Funds since 2007/2008.

Nigerian issues are far beyond a single book. But I will do my best because Nigeria must be better. In 2018, I convened the Solution Summit to find a solution to National programs. As I did not have enough resources, most of the programs of Solution Summit Nigeria were not executed as planned. But we were able to tap from the minds of well-meaning Nigerians who wanted a change in the polity. Since 2018, I have also championed a one-minute prayers for Nigeria by Nigerians on the first of every month. You may not have heard of this as this is primarily through the

WhatsApp platform, but many progressive Nigerians have been praying for Nigeria. Recently, I registered Health Strategies, Solutions and Systems (HS3) to help rebuild the Nigerian healthcare system.

This book may not proffer popular solutions to the issues and challenges of the nation. Nevertheless, the solutions identified and discussed here, if and when well implemented will save Nigeria from total destruction – a journey that has long started with diverse devastating activities seen across the length and breathe of Nigeria.

To rebuild Nigeria, we need new strategies, new solutions and new systems. Join me as together we tell ourselves the truths and join hands to rebuild this giant of Africa.

This is not a book of many words but a book of strategies, solutions and systems that will help rebuild the broken walls, broken heart and broken life of Nigeria.

NIGEIRA shall rise again. And that begins right now.

Chapter 1

The Problems and Challenges of Nigeria

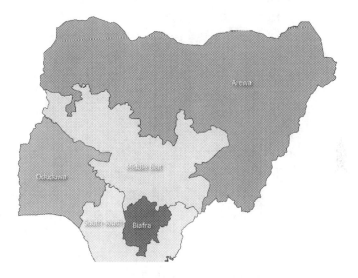

Nigeria has several challenges. Some of these challenges have existed for over 100 years. A few just came to limelight some years ago. These problems affect the politics, economy, culture and all departments of national well-being. Let us take a look at some of the critical challenges and problems facing Nigeria.

1. **The Amalgamation:** The amalgamation by Lord Lugard was a mistake. Joining the northern and southern protectorates was a major mistake. What informed this decision is not known nor shared till date other than for the interest of the British colonial masters. They wanted to reduce the cost of governance, the number of people posted to Nigeria and the impact of this on their economy. The Nigerian people were not asked what they wanted but the desires of the masters were foisted on Nigerians – whether they liked it not. For over 100 years, Nigerians have endured this – even against their will.

   The amalgamation brought together over 350 different languages and cultures and over 250 tribes into what is known today as Nigeria. It also brought together under one roof people from the north and south despite the fact that they had nothing – and I mean with all sense of modesty – absolutely nothing in common. The amalgamation was the first cardinal mistake in the history of Nigeria.

   Since amalgamation, Nigerians have tried to make this unholy marriage work – but to no avail. This led to the next major problem – independence.

2. **The Independence:** Nigerian leaders thought that the British leadership was the challenge they had prior to independence and thus agitated for, and got independence from the British in October 1, 1960. But the decay of the nation showed that this was a wrong assumption. At independence, to maintain balance, leaders were chosen from both the northern and southern part Nigeria – Prime Minister went to the north, while the President went to the south. The differences in culture and religion, the lack of core values and distrust manifested almost immediately resulting in the first coup d'etat in 1966 that resulted in the death of several top leaders and finally led to mass murder of the southerners in the north and the civil war between 1966 - 1970. The independence when the nation was not ripe for self-governance – was the next major problem Nigeria faced.

3. **The Coup Plots:** The first coup plot by the military which was ill advised occurred early in the life of the republic of Nigeria. This coup was followed by another coup and both led to the death of top military leaders and inhuman death of national leaders. Since the first coup plot, Nigeria has remained a victim of several other national and regional coup plots which had worsened the issues against national cohesion and peace. None of the coup plots

was well informed bringing about distrust in the military and sometimes, death of innocent people.

4. **The Civil War:** Following the mass murders of the Igbos and people from the South East in the North, Col Emeka Odumegwu Ojukwu and Lt Col Yakubu Gowon failed to agree on the best solution (e.g. Aburi Accord) which led to a preventable civil war that destroyed the lives of over 3 million people from south eastern Nigeria. The civil war lasted for about three years, hunger was used as weapon to kill innocent children and support for the south easterners was blocked to ensure the full impact of the war. Post-civil war, although there was no winner nor loser, the property and resources of Biafrans were confiscated and shared as abandoned properties. All their resources were taken by the state and a painful 20 pounds was given to them instead of their millions in the bank. Above all, the international and national conglomerates were sold to those who could afford them at the expense of these people who were deliberately refranchised by the government.

5. **The Natural Resources:** Nigeria is blessed with several mineral resources, and there is no part of the nation without unique natural resources. Before the discovery of crude oil,

the groundnut pyramids of the north, onion and cocoa were the key exports of the nation. Agricultural products were the key export and foreign exchange earner for Nigeria. But crude oil was found in the Niger Delta in 1950s and this changed the entire national dynamics. All eyes were now fixed only on the crude to the negligence of the former source of foreign exchange earners. This shift led to another economic war between the north and south – with most of the southern oil wells owned by the northerners. Advocacy for change and equal treatment led to the death of many including Ken Saro Wiwa and the Ogoni team. Gas flaring, air pollution, sea contamination and loss of farm lands in the oil rich areas of Nigeria without adequate compensation has remained another key challenge of the giant of Africa. And, although there are natural resources in the north – like Gold in Zamfara, these are nationally mined and shared like the Oil in the Niger Delta. Solid mineral mining and exploitation in the north has also led to chemical poisoning of ground water and the death of children.

6. **The Geography and Topography:** Nigeria is blessed with an excellent geography and topography with minimal natural disasters. But while we have the lush green vegetation in the south, the north has the challenges

of desertification. Vegetable and plantation flourish in the south, while animal husbandry is the key activities seen in the north – especially among the mobile Fulani population. As desert encroaches into the northern states, there is the need for downward migration to green zones leading to the current crisis in most middle belt region between farmers and Fulani herdsmen. As the herds men must feed their flocks, community crisis, community invasion and community ejection have become the order of the day; and have caused in some states, mass murders and mass burials like in Benue state.

7. **The Beliefs and Religious Systems:** Nigeria has three main belief systems – Christianity, Islam and Traditional or African. Of these, while Christianity believes in peaceful evangelism, Islam believes in Holy War. This has given rise to a number of uprising and Jihads including the ongoing imbrued – Boko Haram that has killed over 10,000 people, sacked 1000 communities and burnt hundreds of churches. Today, there is massive distrust and churches, mosque, and church/Moslem leaders are kidnapped, killed and burnt as part of the ongoing crisis across the northern part of Nigeria. The Niger Delta is not spared with so much kidnappings, destructions of oil installations

and economic devastation. Another major rising belief system that is working against the nation is the killer Fulani herdsmen. Although they have been recognized as a major terrorist group in the world, the nation of Nigeria is still treating them with kid gloves, trying to rehabilitate them along with Boko Haram converts and reintegrating them into the system and the military. However, the Indigenous People of Biafra (IPOB), and most recently, the *Amotekun* as a regional police. This has triggered various reactions from several quarters,

8. **The Educational Systems:** The Nigerian educational system is diverse with both Western, Christian and Islamic studies allowed. So, we have people who have three different orientations working in the same system, to achieve same or divergent goals. While graduates of western and Islamic studies can be found in all departments of national life, graduates of Christian studies are only seen preaching the word and managing churches. Also, while Islam allows for four wives and many children, Christianity frowns at more than one wife, and Christian wives are too westernized to have more than 3 – 4 children. This has resulted in biological skewing of the curve with Islam

likely becoming the predominant language and culture in 30 to 50 years' time.

9. **The Politics of Number and British Lies:** Facts emerging from the archive revealed that Nigeria was amalgamated on lies, built on lies and sustained by lies before, during and immediately after the colonial period. It is like the world was told lies in all things – the size of the nation, the population, the resources, the people and every other thing. Just before the British handed over government to Nigerians at independence, they took a count of Nigeria and gave the bigger proportion of the figure to the northerners. This has been sustained for over 50 years resulting in unbalanced multiplication of states, LGAs and Wards. Whereas Lagos had 12 Local Government Areas in 1996 and has remained the same, Kano has given birth to three other states and many new LGAs and Wards. To therefore get higher subvention and attention, figures are manipulated and national census figures is never accurate. This has caused about unacceptable results every time a census is done. This number politics is hindering proper accreditation of voters, national numbering system and several other progressive interventions in Nigeria.

10. **The Fake Support by the World Super Powers:** Since independence, Nigeria has enjoyed supports from many nations of the world including the United States, the United Kingdom, China, Saudi Arabia, etc. Most of these helps came in the form of grants, loans, and facilities. Recent discoveries are showing that there may be more supports from unnamed nations for some not too noble causes. These supports may be responsible for the numerous crisis Nigeria is facing, the funding of Boko Haram and killer Fulani Herdsmen, and several other national disasters. In addition, loans and grants from some countries are utilized by these countries in Nigeria to build infrastructures such as roads, railways, airports, etc. to their own standards and cost, and Nigeria is billed to pay with huge interest.

11. **Corruption:** I have deliberately left this for the last as, although everyone mentions this first, what they refer to as corruption is not as important as people may make it sound - in my own views. Why? Because corruption is fuelled by all the factors discussed above. There will be little or no corruption if there was no colonization, amalgamation, faulty independence, multiple coup plots, deadly civil war with genocide and man's wickedness to others, exploitation of natural resources,

non-viable educational systems, and religious acrimony, politics of fake numbers and lies, and lopsided support from world powers. Corruption is foreign to Nigeria and was introduced to Nigeria by colonial masters who established Nigeria on corruption, sustained her on corruption, and want to continue to perpetuate these corruption practices.

The real Corruption in my view is not the mere demands for money before files are moved, not the police asking for bribes on our highways and in state roads, not the change of figures in the annual budgets of the state, parastatals, ministries and agencies, ALTHOUGH ALL THESE ARE WRONG and should not be condoned. The real corruption in Nigeria is the injustice meted to the oil producing regions of Nigeria where oil belonging to them are explored, exploited and channelled to develop other parts of Nigeria while the real owners wallow in abject poverty, environmental pollution and negligence. The real corruption is the giving of oil wells to people who have nothing at stake concerning the wells at the expense of the real owners of the Niger Delta. For instance, from available records, most wells are owned by northerners while the indigenes of the oil producing state services them. This was a product of oil well allocation by the military without any resort to the constitution of the nation. The real corruption is the oil cabals who make billions from just allocating vehicles to pick up refined products, importing what we can produce and exploiting Nigeria with subsidy that does not exist. The real corruption is the foreign exchange cabal that take national resources at give-away exchange rate as importers while exchanging the same money at the parallel market making millions in few minutes. The real corruption is the giving of import licences to companies that are not importing anything by government just to have access to foreign exchange at government approved low prices. The real corruption is the government sponsored terrorism with funded helicopters dropping food and equipment to Boko Haram, with the military securing hooligans and terrorist after an attack and government asking that they be not killed but rehabilitated. The real corruption is seen in government giving over 100 billion naira to a group to help them buy more equipment to kill more people, pay their evil bills and turn Nigeria into a war zone. These are the real corruption!

Corruption also perpetuates the decadence through the factors discussed in Chapter 2 of this book. Corruption is an enemy of national development and works against the development and peace of Nigeria.

Corruption corrodes national peace and security. Unfortunately, the people that shout corruption most are also the authors of corruption, the powers sustaining corruption and the benefactors of corruption.

You can see that the problems of Nigeria started before amalgamation and has continued to date. Solving the problem without looking at the core and root causes is a wasted effort. This has failed before and will continue to fail. Thus, the need for this root cause analysis.

Study Report 1:
Demographics of Responders
and Problems of Nigeria

Of the 99 respondents that were analysed, over 65.66% were males; 47.96% were between 21- 40 years while the rest (52.04%) were above 40 years. Also, 60.61% had post graduate qualifications. The rest had O level (4.04%) and Graduate (35.35%) qualifications.

Participants were drawn from all the geopolitical zones although more than half (55.56%) came from the South East. Other participants came from South-South (15.15%), South West (8.08%), North East (3.03%), North West (9.09%) and North Central (9.09%). While 88.79% were Christians, the rest Moslems.

The very large post graduate, South-East and Christian Respondents informed the need to conduct a second survey to minimize any bias resulting from this select group of Nigerians.

Over 301 problems and challenges were identified following the question, "What do you think are the 3 key problems or challenges in Nigeria as a nation?" (Appendix 1). These problems and challenges were classified into 36 groups. Corruption, insecurity and poor/bad leadership and administration topped the list.

The top common problems in Nigeria according to all responders are;

Problem or Challenge	Percentage
Corruption	37
Insecurity	36
Poor/Bad Leadership	33
Tribalism/Ethnicity	25
Religious Intolerance	21
Ignorance/Illiteracy	21
Unemployment	16
Poverty/Hunger	11
Selfishness/Greed	11
Politics	10
Weak institution	10

Some respondents said,

"The leadership of the country know what to do but they won't do it because they benefit more from the rot much more than they would have in an organized setting"

"The followership is largely uniformed, daft, gullible and timid...Uninformed Political Class that does have a clue on how to liberate us from WHITE PEOPLE'S strangle Economic Grip"

"There are laws but, we really don't have independent judiciary"

"Some tribes think they *(sic are)* better off than some because they have a larger population."

"Dearth of good economic policies, or lack of will to implement same."
"Low regard for competence and excellence, but reliance on sycophancy and nepotism"

"Key problems: Plenty *(sic Many)* politician (few leaders), mistrust between the people leading and those being led, perception of 'let me grab my own (National) cake' before it finishes, failed electoral system that cannot guarantee or bring aboard capable leaders, politicians with zero leadership to lead, politicians with no zeal to get trained to lead, too many selfish aspirations."

These show that Nigeria has a problem, and pretending to be free of problems has not and will not solve them for us.

To the question, *"What do you think are the three (3) root cause(s) of these problems?",* 304 different root causes were mentioned and these were classified into 39 different groups Greed and Selfishness (including covetousness, self-interest), Corruption, and Ignorance and Illiteracy topped the list (Appendix 2)

The root causes according to the respondents are

Root Causes	Percentage
Poor/Bad Leadership	40
Selfishness/Greed	40
Corruption	31
Ignorance/Illiteracy	22
Religious Intolerance/fanaticism	21
Tribalism/Ethnicity	19
Poor educational practices	19
Politics including lack of Political will	18
Poverty/Hunger	12
Failed/Weak systems including Judiciary and electoral	12
Mediocratic system	5

Some participants said,

"Bad Administration and lack of interest in research for green energy, and over dependence on the western world."

"Indifference (sic -Indifferent) attitude by the citizens and lack of mitigation strategies by the government."

"Illiterate (sic – illiterates) who don't know they have rights or can have a better life than the current one that have been given to them by corrupt politicians."

"Lack of good education amongst the ruling class and vast majority of the citizens."

"Poor and weak institutions to prevent corruption and lack of political will to implement policies."

"Everybody wants the "National Cake", greed and selfishness."

"Institutions of learning have become business centres, and money-making ventures, parents now believe in settlement even to pass SSCE and to gain admission, lecturers and teachers are no longer dedicated as before."

"No value for lives in Nigeria, our security outfits are invaded by politicians in uniform."

"Majority of Nigerians are uneducated and there are no standards in all the various sectors of the country."

"The high level of insecurity is also a consequence of the over-concentration of power at the centre."

"Inadequate political will to fund compulsory vocational and technical education."

"The black-man's blind adherence to religions detrimental to his race."

Pulse and Reflect
Is Nigeria A Failed State?

As the years roll by, recent occurrences in Nigeria have led to my reflection on the above topic – Is Nigeria a failed State?

1. Nigerian women and girls were raped, murdered and refrigerated, and buried without a comment from the government, Nigerian embassies or the world at large.

2. Nigerians have been profiled and sold as slaves for less than $400 in Libya. A significant number work as slaves or are forced into prostitution without an outcry from anybody in Nigeria – including the government.

3. Majority of people attempting to enter Europe and dying in the Mediterranean are Nigerians. Some have stayed over 2 years on the way (some in Sahara desert), many are working in unhealthy jobs to pay for their journey, some ladies have gotten pregnant and delivered children while on transit, and majority have died. Still there is no official comment from the government or any national outcry.

Here in Nigeria,

1. Boko Haram is killing, maiming and destroying homes, communities and societies; and the media is deadly silent. We only get piecemeal information from the social media. And the law provides for freedom of information and press.

2. Innocent people are kidnapped or abducted and released only after several millions have exchanged hands. Yet we have the police, Civil Defence, and army.

3. People are paying taxes to government, but still provide their own roads, bridges, water and electricity.

4. Millions of innocent children in North East and the Internally Displaced People's Camps across the nation are killed by hunger on a daily basis. This has necessitated the sales of children in some camps for less than N100,000.00 per child – without any outcry.

5. Child abuse – physical, emotional and sexual – is at an all-time high as children are made to do the work adults will not do, forced to become income earners for their families, and several are trafficked out of Nigeria for sex trade – without any official outcry.

6. People (including high profile personalities) get 'missing' and nobody ever investigates.

All these are happenings, some are reported, others are not and nobody is saying anything.
Nigerians still go about their normal duties as if all is well. We know that all is not well in Nigeria and with Nigeria.

Is Nigeria a failed State? This is the time for us all to sit down and discuss.

Chapter 2

The Perpetuating Factors

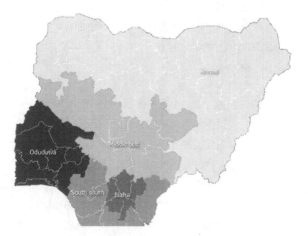

The causes enumerated above and many others not identified here led to the present deteriorated state of Nigeria, although they worked in collusion with a number of perpetuating factors. These include;

1. **Poor and Unhealthy Politics:** In Nigeria there is the unhealthy politics of divide and rule, in addition, we have a lot of politics of

no value. Some people across the nation are full time politicians and can do anything and everything to remain relevant. They bow to forces, kneel before altars, and go into covenant to attain a position, win an election or be appointed into an office.

Also, the lies of number of national strengths have made some segments believe that without power, they cannot survive – which is completely untrue. The do or die nature of Nigerian politics has regularly led to violence at elections resulting in destruction of lives and properties of people, states and nation at large.

The lack of political philosophy of politicians has made them become prostitutes and willing to sleep with any and every one to achieve their primary goal of relevance. The absence of decent political parties has led to the creation of tens to hundreds of parties that are neither grounded nor focused enough to make any impact in the national political landscape. The absence of decent politicians with values has made Nigerian politics an all comer's affairs. This poor and unhealthy political environment has sustained the weaknesses that began from amalgamation, building massive distrust, communal clashes, and public unrest. The dependence of the judiciary - which is the last hope of the ordinary man – to the Executive has made the issues worse. There is the need to review the current political practices if Nigeria must move forward.

2. **Unconstitutional Constitution:** Nigeria is governed currently by the 1999 constitution which is actually an unconstitutional constitution produced by the military which has no democratic right to produce one. By right, Nigeria should still be operating the 1963 constitution which gave birth to the republic and the regions. The 1963 came into force on 1st of October, 1963 and continued in operation until the military coup of 1966 which overthrew Nigeria's democratic institutions. The 1999 constitution was adopted after the 1979 and 1993 constitution that turned Nigeria into a presidential system following the American style of democracy, and started the Fourth Republic of Nigeria. The 1979, 1993 and 1999 constitutions added so much into the constitution that has over the years hindered development, added to the distrust and supported religious challenges, problems and conflicts. The implementation of this unconstitutional constitution is one of the core perpetuating factors of Nigerian crisis.

3. **Force of Poverty and Hunger:** Poverty and hunger were used as weapons of war against the Biafrans in Nigeria. In recent days, poverty and hunger have also been used against the minority to make them do the will of the wealthy and the power that be. Poverty is used to keep people subjective. So, today, Nigeria is described as the poverty capital of the world with over 72% of Nigerians living below the poverty line. Today, poverty is still being used to keep people subservient to the government and to the wealthy as people are unemployed, the employed are not being paid liveable wages, salaries are not paid on time, workers are wrongly treated and abused, and the unqualified are employed to supervise the qualified. All these result in poor productivity, improved poverty and hunger across the nation. The deliberately created large population of poor and very poor people in the system has led to an insecure nation where there are all manner of evils including kidnapping, armed robbery, intentional rapes and murders, even arsons, massive community rampage and looting.

4. **Intertribal Disharmony and Acrimony:** Distrust and lack of harmony between several tribes, cultures and tongues is another perpetrating factor. While Hausa men cannot in all sincerity trust a Yoruba or Igbo men,

the same is the case with the other tribes. Since civil war, an Igbo man is not trusted to hold strategic positions in the military or presidency. And when they do, they are surrounded with people of other tribes. Currently, only one tribe - the Fulani - holds all the strategic military and security position as the incumbent president cannot trust people from other tribes and tongues. Intertribal distrust and challenges result in tribal and communal wars, conflicts and crisis. These have led to multiple internally displaced peoples' camps across Nigeria - especially in the north east where Boko Haram holds sway. This challenge is further fuelled by the inequity in the system leading to skewed treatment of people from different tribes, tongues and cultures.

1. **Unhealthy Policies and Legislations:** Nigeria is still operating unhealthy policies and legislations that are biased, full of dishonest statements and skewed to a particular region. Not addressing this makes a segment of Nigerians feel as second-class citizens and this fuels injustice, conflicts and dissatisfaction with the system. Furthermore, the absence of true federalism due to the 1999 constitution makes regional development impossible as all segments of the nation must report to a supreme leader in the person of

the President. These polices and legislation hinder innovation, creativity, and out of the box thinking as anything outside the approved events, activities or programs are seen as treasonable offences.

2. **Continued Suspicion Between Tribes and Cultures:** This is one major perpetrating factor for the current national crisis. Groups do not trust each other anymore. Everyone is afraid of the next and on the lookout for possible reprisal attacks or conflicts. Social media has worsened this as fake news are shared and they go viral within hours. Doing business with people who are not from your tribe now is dangerous. Food stuff are *chemicalized* and sometimes out rightly poisoned. Families are killed and top leaders burnt in their houses. Stakeholders are kidnapped and outrageous sums called for their ransom and if not paid on time, they are killed. Women and young girls are raped as they go to farm and their farm produced destroyed, sometimes by cattle and herdsmen. Churches are burnt and communities are completely killed and their houses burnt for no reason other than tribal, cultural or religious differences. These have put into the hearts and mind of people fear and heightened suspicion between tribes and cultures and is the most prominent perpetuating factor of the continued

decadence in Nigeria. This suspicion has actually extended to include intra-tribal and intracultural – but this is not as devastating as intertribal and inter-cultural suspicion.

3. **Unequal Distribution of Natural Resources:** Unequal distribution of resources like the crude oil is another perpetuating factor. Just because the oil is in a particular part of Nigeria, resources from this region is used to develop other regions without adequate compensation to the owners of the resources. Moreover, other resources (like gold and other solid minerals) located in other regions are not equally distributed to solve the problems of others. This has resulted in dissatisfaction with the system and movements for the emancipation, freedom or ever complete dissociation from the Nigerian project. It is actually amazing that some regions have neglected their own resources in their search to exploit the resources of other regions. In addition, sometimes, forces including violence and deaths are being used to dislodge people's rights and inheritances.

4. **Leadership Imbalance:** Since after the civil war, leadership of the Nigerian state has become the prerogative of a particular segment of the nation. It is their right to rule, to determine who rules, and to decide

who occupies what position in government, parastatals and all the various government agencies and ministries. When this is not done, there will be unholy war to destabilize the system and make it ungovernable. Leadership imbalance is also seen in the creation of various cabals within and outside the government system, forcing their opinions and plans on others and forcefully removing any obstacle on their way – be it human or otherwise. The most affected are the minority tribes that do not have the number or finances to fight the major tribes. Such minor tribes benefit from tokenism from the major tribes. When such offers are given and accepted, the person ends up serving as a stooge for the individuals or groups who offered the position. We also see people today buy positions with very huge sums of money or pay their ways into elective positions – even to the point of buying the supreme court of the land. These unequal balances perpetuate evil in the land.

5. **Inequity and Injustice in Civil Service, Judiciary and Legislative:** Although Nigeria has the Federal/National Character Commission established by Act No 34 of 1996 to implement and enforce the Federal Character Principle of fairness and equity in the distribution of public posts and socio-economic infrastructures among the various

federating units of the Federal Republic of Nigeria, appointment and promotion into strategic positions in Nigeria is still very biased and skewed to the north. Equal number of people from the various regions or states may be employed, but promotion, retirement and even removal from the system does not follow the Federal Character pattern. This makes it easy for a particular tribe, culture of religion to have a comparative advantage over others as you rise in the cadre to management levels. Today, it is only people from one region that occupy most sensitive positions in the country with most of their classmates retired from active service to pave way for their promotions. The most annoying part of this is that there is no system in place to justify the level of biased promotions, retirement or appointments seen in the nation. The inequity is worse in the armed forces where the level of bias and skewness is unbelievable and sad. This is one of the perpetuating factors causing distrust and insecurity in the nation.

6. **Porous Borders:** The borders are very porous – especially in the northern parts of the country. When they are closed (as it happened in 2019/2020), they are closed against legitimate businessmen and women who are involved in legitimate trade. The porous borders allow anything and everything

into the country including contraband goods. The porosity of the borders also allows foreign nationals to come into the nation to cause problems – which is one of the reasons immigration visa was banned in Nigeria to the United States of America. With porous borders, any idiot can come into Nigeria and claim to be a Nigerian what he or she needs is a letter from the hungry stricken local government areas which can be gotten with less than 500 naira. The porous borders also make it easy for criminals to leave Nigeria without any problems at all. The recent return of Nnamdi Kalu for the burial of his parents and his exit without federal intervention shows that even highly profiled individuals can come in and leave without the security agents noticing their movements in and out of Nigeria.

7. **Poor Documentation of People and Things:** Unlike in developed countries of the world, there is poor documentation of people and properties in Nigeria. Very few Nigerians have a National Identity card and number. Those that have may also have driver's licences and international passport with different details and addresses. People can have more than one national identity card or voters' card without any consequences in Nigeria. Also, houses, roads and communities

are not properly numbered and majority of the streets in communities are without real identities. Thus, description of locations are usually with all manner of strategic landmarks like behind the market, by the warehouse, around the transformer, adjacent to the school, etc. these are also seen even in major towns like Abuja, Lagos, Port Harcourt, Kano and Enugu.

Where we have some form of documentation, there is usually confusion on what comes first - First Name or Surname. So, Danjuma Shehu may or may not be the same person as Shehu Danjuma. Similarly, middle names are used sparingly. So, the same person may have his name written as Shehu Danjuma, Danjuma Shehu, Shehu U Danjuma, Danjuma U Shehu, and Danjuma Shehu U. These levels of poor documentations make triangulation of information practically impossible, even when desired and funded.

8. **Wrong Governmental Policies and Programs:** Let me end this segment by discussing these. These policies such as the Land Use Degree. Oil well allocation, etc. are major perpetrators of evil in Nigeria resulting in the decadence of the nation. Policies that allow a fully grown man to marry a child leading to vesico-vaginal fistula, children

to attend Almajiri Schools in exchange for formal education, institutionalize joblessness and support oil well allocation to individuals including someone's girlfriend; and monopoly in essential goods and services such as cement, salt, flour, etc. perpetuate national decadence.

These are the common perpetuating factors leading to massive decay of Nigeria as a nation. If I am asked, I would say that the high level of distrust between different ethnic groups followed by global insecurity are the worst things that ever happened to Nigeria and Nigerians. Some may think I am wrong. But this is why there is no progress, no development, and no long-term plans as everyone is looking for what to grab, steal, appropriate or destroy.

What can we do to make Nigeria a better nation? Before I attempt to answer this vital question, let us look at effects and impacts of these root causes and the perpetuating factors.

Survey Report 2:
Perpetuating Factors

To the question, "What do you think are the three (3) main perpetuating factors sustaining these problems and challenges?", 304 possible factors were identified, and these are grouped into 40 classes. Bad administration and poor leadership, ignorance (or illiteracy) and greed/selfishness topped the list as shown in Appendix 3

Top perpetuating factors include

Perpetuating Factors	Percentage
Poor/Bad Leadership	32
Ignorance/Illiteracy	25
Selfishness/Greed	24
Tribalism/Ethnicity	22
Religious Intolerance and Fanaticism	22
Corruption	20
Poverty/Hunger	17
Mind-set including insincerity and sycophancy	15
Failed Judiciary system	15
Politics including politics without ideology	13
Failed Judiciary system	9

Poor citizens engagement and awareness	9

Some responders said,

"Unwillingness of the government to review our educational system and design our own based on our needs."

"In Nigeria we have so many individuals more powerful than the institutions of government."

"The "mortal" fear of allowing devolution of powers to the federating units by the core north."

"While there's no community in world without some level of insecurity, the case of Nigeria has been worsened by the desire of the Fulani oligarch to dominate the sociocultural and political space in the entire country."

"In the North, it is feudalism; in the South, it is over-dependence on paper qualification."

"'Feeding bottle' federalism where every state and LGA have to go to Abuja for handouts."

"Infrastructural deficit including power, roads, railways."

"One section of the country feels has a sense of entitlement and lordship over other parts of Nigeria."

Pulse and Reflect:
Owerri: Home of Projects…
but No Project Management

All over Imo State are products of the excellent vision of one time governor, Owelle Rochas Okoroacha. From the State capital to the hinder-lands, houses, offices, roads, hospitals, women center, etc. are either under construction or completed. Every year, the then Governor Okoroacha hosted workers and several meetings in the Hero's Square. There is also a children's recreation center, a dialysis center, etc.

Going through Owerri, one will be amazed by the legacies of an active Governor, who is working tirelessly to leave his feet in the sand of time. For Imo State indigenes who travelled out of the state and have been away for more than a year, they may miss their way in the current State capital due to new roads opened by Owelle Rochas Okoroacha. Some of the building are colourful and tastefully designed, some of the street decorations are unique. Truly, Owelle Rochas Okoroacha has been very active designing, developing and deploying projects.

Nonetheless, these did not last. If you transverse the major roads (old and new), you will see the outcome of functional leadership, but most of the new roads were full of several potholes few months after their construction, making driving through them difficult. Completed building looked old and worn out just because the wrong paints were used. In some buildings, the finishing were falling apart. The ex-Governor's team of project managers were active implementing projects without the requisite skills and competencies for project management.

Truly, the Governor worked. Yet, there were several avoidable weaknesses in his products. These weaknesses resulted from the unskillfulness of the project management team in the art of project management. When projects are not well planned, designed, developed and deployed, they become a major challenge to the future generation. Repairing, standardizing and even upgrading is usually more expensive than doing the right thing at first. Quality is better (and cheaper) ensured at the construction phase than after work has been done!

The governor's project management team (PMT) needed project management skills. Projects should be built to last. Projects should be built to meet the quality standards and criteria of the Standard Organization of Nigeria (SON), Nigeria Society of Engineers (NSE), and several other regulating bodies in Nigeria. The Governor should not only think of doing new things, but building to last. Some roads built by Chief Sam Mbakwe in the late 70s, and early 80s are still standing strong. Meanwhile, roads built in less than 12 months are already falling apart. Sustainability should be our watchword!

For instance, building and dismantling is a colossal waste of resources – time, money and manpower. Projects should be planned, implemented according to plan and monitored to ensure that every segment of the project meet (and if possible exceeds) the set quality standards, satisfies the owners and users of the projects and are executed in a most effective and efficient manner.

Buildings, constructions, and even developments that are not planned, monitored and evaluated will not yield the right kind of results. We need to use the available resources effectively and efficiently. We need to ensure sustainable investment in the State. We need to build and construct things that add value to the lives of the people. We need to ensure functionality of these projects even after the administration. We need life changing policies, products and projections.

Building and construction are, therefore, not just enough. We need investments that make sense.

Chapter 3

The Effects and Impacts

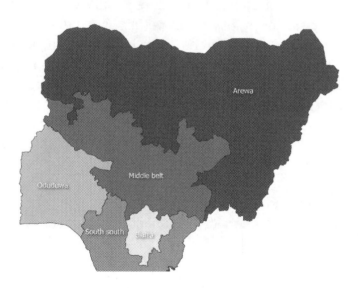

The various challenges Nigeria is facing have had several negative consequences on the growth and development of the nation. These are very disturbing and destabilizing for a nation with so much potentials that today, people see Nigeria as a failed nation. I see the country as sitting on time bomb about to explode. Leaving Nigeria to live in another country may sound good, but this is my nation where I belong and definitely, I will always love to be here to do the things I love most - building people and the nation. But with the current level of unrest, conflicts, kidnapping and ritual killings, one is not sure if staying back is the best option. Below are some of the effects and impacts of the various root and perpetuating factors mentioned above.

1. **Multiple and Unabated Crisis and Conflicts:** Crisis are triggered by circumstances, but sustained for a purpose. Nigeria's current crisis and conflicts are funded and sustained to achieve a hidden agenda. We know it as the blame cannot be solely on herdsmen, or the perpetuators.

   Communal crisis and conflicts, religious crisis including Boko Haram and killer Fulani herdsmen attacks has since 2003 graduated from mere skirmishes to daily occurrence across the nation. Today, one is waiting to hear where next they attacked. Even the military has stopped reporting their loses, media houses have been banned unofficially from reporting the carnages and social media is being monitored and people arrested for posting eye witness reports. It is not also uncommon to see government officials openly denying and refuting an eye witness report or claiming that it happened several years before, but the facts stare us daily in the face. Nigeria is in trouble! Communities in the North East are uprooted daily by Boko Haram. Pregnant women are raped and sliced by killer Fulani Herdsmen. Kidnapping is rampant in all major roads across the nation. Innocent people are victims of senseless shootings by Fulani herdsmen to motorist along the travel corridors. Armed robbery is common and perpetuated by jobless Fulani and immigrants into the nation. Fulani herdsmen fight with farmers in the middle belts is also common. In the south (east, west and south-south), the rapid migration of the Fulani herdsmen and the attendant conflicts is becoming unbelievable. The social media is awash with video clips of killings, slaughtering and burning of people in the name of their gods and with their faces to the camera. And the government is doing nothing about it.

Recently, I watched a painful video of mass slaughter and shared it with a top General in the Nigerian Army to confirm the origin and authenticity of the video. In response to the initial and my subsequent questions, he said,

"Nobody is listening to the voice of wisdom and the cry of the people of NE (North East). The situation is not good at all…No one can

predict what the future holds, but it's up to the government to act decisively...My brother, we need to do more as a nation."

This is where we are as a nation – nobody is listening, the situation is not good at all, no one can predict, we need to do more as a nation. Yes, we need to do more as thousands of people have lost their lives, families, communities and farmlands. We have lost churches, schools, markets, government buildings, community recreation facilities, etc. We have lost major income generating companies and industries to these crisis and conflicts. Many investors have had to leave Nigeria as it was not safe to do business again in Nigeria. Crisis, conflicts and clashes have messed up our dear nation – and the government is not doing anything about it.

2. **Poor Development and Deteriorating Infrastructures:** Chaos in a system is bad as it effects the productively, effectiveness and efficiency of the system. But as people benefit from it, it is sustained and sometimes actively stimulated. This is the case for our dear nation – Nigeria.

As I write this today, 28/02/2020, Nigeria confirmed her first case of Coronavirus (COVID-19) yesterday. This was an Italian national on a trip to Nigeria. The questions on the lips of all Nigerians are; (1) Is Nigeria ready for another outbreak? (2) Were Nigerians well prepared and sensitized before the outbreak was confirmed? And (3) Are our systems and infrastructures able to handle this outbreak. The honest answer to the three questions is NO. The question therefore is why?

Like the healthcare system, Nigeria has very poor and deteriorating infrastructures. This is seen across all sectors of the economy – health, education, commerce, power, industry, roads, agricultures, etc. The excellent schools and facilities built by our fathers are not maintained. The new ones commenced are not completed. Till date, over 60 percent of Nigerians do not have access to good and potable water supply, electricity and road networks. Over 75% do not have access to quality healthcare services and a few who have suffered from catastrophic health expenditure as they pay for their health from their pockets. Sleeping at night with electricity is a luxury the power holding company cannot give to majority of the people. The nation is littered with abandoned projects, poorly completed buildings and collapsed structures. These are part of the consequences of the challenges identified above which are perpetuated by several factors including corruption as government contracts are not properly executed, roads and other infrastructures are poorly executed and Nigerians who can afford it still send their relations abroad for healthcare, their children to school abroad and spend their holidays in any nation of the world other than Nigeria. Ghana is fast becoming the home of most holiday maker.

Poor development is also facilitated by the near absence of strategic plans for national development, and where they exist, there are non-implementations. It is not unusual to see several strategic plans created, developed and published dumped in the office of the minister several years after it was printed. Thus, the field workers neither have access to then nor understand the content therein, talk less of implementing them. Poor development and decaying infrastructures are also fuelled by bad policies, program and near absence of genuine supervision and monitoring. If we must rebuild Nigeria, these fundamental challenges must be resolved from the roots.

3. **Boko Haram and Other Agents of National Destabilization:** When terrorism exceeds a particular number of days, there is the involvement of key sectors of the economy including the government. This was the assertion of a former Nigerian Head of

State. The current Boko Haram is funded and sustained by highly placed cabals and individuals who gain maximally from the crisis – otherwise where do they get their supplies and resupplies? How come they have better equipment than the military? How come they are never disturbed every time they move in convoys to attack, kill, and kidnap women and children for sex trade? How come they are growing unchecked by anybody? How come they are given preferential treatment among several groups in Nigeria?

Since 2003, Boko Haram has terrorized Nigerians especially those living in North Eastern region of Nigeria. This became worse since 2014 when they kidnapped school children and took them to their hide out. Beyond children, they kill, maim, and destroy houses, people and communities.

Also, Nigeria is faced with Fulani Herdsmen killers who kill, rape, abduct and kidnap people along highways, women and children in their farm lands, and leaders from their communities. These practices have made Nigeria not too safe for majority of people, sacked good companies and industries; and stimulated community crisis.

Political unrest, recent Supreme Court judgements, kidnapping, Lassa fever, and now Coronavirus are other common cases of destabilization. They destabilize the system by instilling fears in people, causing acrimony, stimulating crisis and causing multiple national, regional and local problems.

The recent reintegration of Boko Haram members into the system – especially the military has heightened the fears and concerns of many.

4. **Unhealthy Systems and Structures:** Despite the humongous amount of resources spent yearly by the three tiers of government and the civil service, the systems are not working, and everybody knows this. The executive, legislative and judiciary are all compromised. No one is sure of anything anymore. These are the realities of the day. To be an executive, you have to pay your way through. To win a case, you have to bribe the judges, to be appointed for a position, you have to pay those involved, to get a bill passed, you have to pay your way through from the first reading. Everything requires somebody paying for it illegally.

When monitoring team come to your parastatals, you have to pay for their trips, their accommodation as well as give them enough money if you do not want them to deliberately write a damming report on you.

To defend and approve a budget, you have to show how much of the budget is meant for the legislatives. This is Nigeria!

Is it therefore surprising that the systems and structures of governance, legislation and judgements are unhealthy and decaying? Is it surprising to see the decay in the civil service, private sector and even in the non-governmental organizations? Advocates have compromised, gatekeepers are bought over and every voice you hear has something to gain further making the systems and structures unhealthier and more ineffective.

Unhealthy system and structures have led to several migration of skilled workers to developed nations of the world in their hundreds of thousands to millions; medical tourism with capital flight of over one billion dollars per year; and massive exodus of Nigerians through the north African desert route and the Mediterranean Sea. These have made living in Nigeria, doing business in Nigeria and even travelling to Nigeria very expensive and unfavourable to many.

5. **Population Explosion and Lack of Value for Life:** While some nations are controlling their population, in Nigeria, large families have remained the order of the day. Some give birth like chicken annually and without

any form of restraint. Others marry as many wives as possible bringing into the world children they cannot take care of.

In some parts of Nigeria, some men have 16 to 50 children from different wives. In polygamous homes, women compete for who will have the highest number of children. Majority of these children are poorly cared for resulting in the challenges of children in the street and children of the street. These children miss any form of education – formal and sometimes informal. They are mentored into criminality and co-opted by evil men/ women to do evil for them. For a morsel of bread or a few thousands, they are turned into mercenaries, suicide bombers and highway armed robbers and kidnappers.

This population explosion is coupled with poor value for life, especially among the northern part of Nigeria where death is seen as nothing, killing people for whatever reason seen as normal; and destruction of houses, churches and public infrastructures is the order of the day. The lack of value for life is seen as people are trained to destroy themselves and the lives of others through suicide bombs, banditry and communal conflicts. It is common to see young boys and girls carrying AK 47, killing, decapitating with knives, shooting to kill, and burying people whose only crime maybe their misfortune of being present at the time of the attack.

6. **National Insecurity and all Manner of Evils including Kidnapping:** People are now afraid to travel. Nigerians abroad are afraid of coming home. Nigerians at home are afraid of going to their villages because of massive and large-scale insecurity across the length and breadth of the nation.

   The decadence in the system has resulted in insecurity across the length and breadth of Nigeria. People cannot anymore trust their neighbours, colleagues in offices, fellow passengers and even security guards who they pay to safeguard their homes and families. Travelling by road today is a nightmare and nobody who can afford air travels, will ever try it because of the sporadic appearance of Fulani Herdsmen on the highway shooting, killing and kidnapping. In some parts of Nigeria, it is dangerous to go home because of fear of kidnappers. In some localities, some people sleep with one eye open as attacks by armed robbers, bandits and even invaders are common.

   The level of insecurity has hindered investments by foreigners in Nigeria, cause big organizations to close shops and depart from Nigeria, and made others to scale down operations. The few that remained have had to increase their security expenditure, engage police guards and sometimes move with bullet proof vehicles and massive security formations. This has made doing business in Nigeria more expensive.

7. **Non-functional Systems and Abandoned Projects:** Non-functional systems and abandoned projects are evidence of poor planning, programming and execution. They are also pointers to non-continuity by subsequent governments of the project commissioned by their predecessors.

The national landscape is littered with these non-functional systems and abandoned projects including those that could completely change the nation and improve her economy. Projects started by previous governments are abandoned and new ones started as there are no continuity in government. Systems are deliberately destroyed to allow for malpractices and unconscionable undertaking. People burn offices, servers are tampered with and document repositories are destroyed to hide evidence of their evil practices. New governments see uncompleted projects as not theirs and thus go ahead to award new ones. It is a cycle of poor, ineffective and inefficient practices. Majority of these are initiated and sustained by the factors enumerated above including selfishness in government, lack of leadership and management skills and undue influence of god fathers and financiers of political movements.

The educational and health infrastructures are in shamble; a ghost of what they should have been. The wealthy and privileged prefer to send their children/wards to colleges abroad, and going for medical check-up and treatment there as death rates in our facilities are at an all-time high. I have friends who have been on admission now for over a year resulting from medical malpractice due to lack of relevant equipment and facilities. This decadence is seen in all sectors of the economy and national life.

8. **Debt Ridden Economy:** Debts may look attractive, but they are enemies of national growth. Leaders use the available resources to services debts rather than using the same to provide amenities such as water, electricity, security, healthcare, jobs, etc. for the people who they serve.

Some leaders love debts. They collect these monies knowing that they will not be the ones that will pay them off. They collect, use, steal some, misappropriate others and blame their predecessors for their errors and ineffectiveness. Although President Obasanjo delivered Nigeria from foreign debts, our current debt burden now has risen again to very unacceptable levels. Every year, new loans are accessed putting Nigeria into more difficult situation and position. The painful part of this cycle of debts, debt management/ serving and debt repayment is that one hardly sees what the loans collected were used for. Chinese loans are given to Chinese companies to execute infrastructural projects in Nigeria. IMF and World Bank Loans are used to settle Fulani herdsmen and boko haram, indirectly empowering them with resources to cause more harm. Internal loans are collected as debentures and bonds and used to negotiate for kidnapped children, repairs of the national assembly and president's lodge. Loans are taken from every nook and crannies without any justifiable reason for them. Servicing these debts cause Nigeria the resources it would have used to build healthy and long-lasting infrastructures, pay for the education of her children in school and establish a world class hospital.

9. **Civil Unrest and Engagement:** Workers and communities' unrest in Nigeria is a common occurrence. As I write, I saw a social media video of people with disability asking for their

rights in Lagos Nigeria. Recently, Imo State citizens were on the streets contesting the Supreme Court judgement that removed their dully elected Governor and replaced him with another. Doctors also are on strike as I write asking for Nigerian University Commission to reverse its stand on Fellowships and PHD. These are just a tip of the iceberg.

Nowadays, people go on strike as they wake up from sleep, go to work or return from work. Strike action in Nigeria could be called on any hour of the day, any day of the week (even on weekends), and any month of the year. Once agreement is reached, workers down their tools and strikes begin.

Also, advocates can mobilize people to demonstrate for any and everything. Recently, Catholics, Christians and Concerned citizens have demonstrated the incessant kidnaps and killings of priests, church leaders and Christians across the nation. They also demonstrated against the burning of churches, refusal to give allocation for church plantings and several other national and local issues.

Strikes in the healthcare system is the most common in Nigeria because of multitude of unions and associations in the sector with diverse interests and demands; and the near absence of effective leadership by the doctors.

Other sectors that commonly go on strike are the oil and gas workers and teachers. The lawyers and accountants went on strike once.

The decadence in Nigeria led to poor wages and salary structures, delayed payment of salaries, non-adherence to agreed terms and condition with workers, absence of working tools, non-modernization of work benches, excessive exposure to risk, poor capacity development programs, inadequate human resources, unhealthy work environment, etc. In the communities, the absence of good leadership, the demand for equity and equality, the need for freedom of association and expression, and the resolve to improve the life of the common man has led to several civil unrest. Recently, a musician, Charly Boy Oputa began a campaign titled "Our MUMU don Do" to draw attention to the lackadaisical attitude of people to issues of national importance.

In a decayed nation like Nigeria, every evil is allowed to happen. Innocent children are slaughtered for rituals. Ladies are killed in hotels and joints. People are trafficked to Middle East and North African for various reasons including prostitution, females are sexually exploited by people they love and respect; or by bandits, terrorists and criminals. Anything and everything goes. This is why a rebuilding is critical and the time has come.

Pause and Reflects
Let's Do Away with the Conspiracy of Silence

Friends, the success of the 50 years commemoration of Biafra on May 30 2017 is a pointer that the season of silence is OVER. I was born towards the end of the civil war and I lost my twin sister probably because of the war, although my parents never told me what killed her!

My father told me many years ago that you do not solve a problem by pretending that it does not exist. He also told me that whatever you hide under the carpet (now rug) will be exposed when the carpet is removed.

The time has come for a round table discussion – not by those who have sold our nation for naught; not by the current representatives or political leaders; but by those who mean well for Nigeria as a nation, the Igbo people, and our children and children's children.

The time for this conversation is NOW! The further we postpone this conversation, the more difficult it becomes to achieve a peaceful resolution with an outcome that will be fully acceptable to all, without bloodshed and conflicts.

The more we delay this conversation, the more we empower the enemies of the nation who love chaos and are already exploiting it to maximize their gains at the expense of the nation.

The more we delay this conversation, the more likely all parties will lose and the nation will suffer. NOW is the time for this long-awaited discussion and conversation.

Can the current leadership of Nigeria muster the needed courage and political will to do what is right? Can they take steps in the right direction to foster real peace and harmony with all parties rejoicing at the end of the day? Could this be the real CHANGE we were promised – a new NIGERIA where everyone has equal rights and privileges, equal opportunities to the nation's resources, and equal access to positions and promotions?

Could this be the real CHANGE where every tribe is proud of who he/she is? Where every tribe has the freedom to develop and maximize their potentials? Where leaders lead the people and not their offices and for their pockets? Where men show and do what men are known for – courage and exemplary leadership?

Could this be the hour for true change where people can associate freely and as they desire, where the voice of the common man is heard and respected; where leaders emerge from the people and are not imposed on them; where the vote of the ordinary man counts in the election of new leaders?

The hour has come. Let us UNITE to UNIFY through honest dialogues, restitutions, real and sincere apologies to those we have wronged – knowingly or otherwise, and strategic road map to a new Nigeria.

Friends let the conversation begin.

Chapter 4

The Strategies, Solutions and Systems

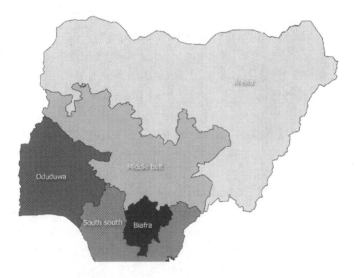

Looking at the cause of the national problems, we can solve a number of them – but not all. For instance, amalgamation took place in 1914. We cannot return to 1914 but we can learn from the experience, deliberately and proactively chart the course of national rebirth. In as much as we cannot change that history, we can grow from it into a nation that makes sense. What we currently have as a nation does NOT make sense at all!

Core national milestones were independence in 1960, republic in 1963, civil war in 1966 and end of civil war in 1970. Also, political assassinations, coup plots, unilateral creation of states and local government areas, oil well allocation, etc. have all augmented the problem, facilitated national quarrels and discords, further fuelling the disharmony in the nation.

In this section, I will be making some usual and unusual suggestions that if accepted and implemented, can make a difference in the nation towards rebuilding the national image, glory and peace.

To rebuild Nigeria, justice is key, so we must start at the root. Let us return to the genesis – the constitution.

1. **1963 Constitutional Review:** We cannot build a just society with an unjust constitution. We cannot rebuild Nigeria running on wrong principles, biased laws and unacceptable policies. To rebuild Nigeria, we must first and foremost review the constitution. This will start with the National Assembly taking a bold step to return Nigeria to the 1963 constitution which is the legal instrument for Nigeria, and begin from there to rebuild the nation. All state and Local Government Areas created by the Military between 1970 and 2020 should

be nullified and a new Nigeria initiated via a democratically elected National Assembly. The constitution review committee will be drawn from the 1963 approved regions for proper regional representation and allowed to modify or upgrade the 1963 constitution. If we need more states and LGAs, it will be their responsibility to recommend and ensure a proper spread across the regions of Nigeria.

I know that this will be a hard nut to crack, but it is the best solution to the national decadence as you do not repair cracked walls by plastering them, but by reviewing and reworking the foundation of the building. The constitutional review will among other things, look at the amalgamation document (if it can be seen) and agree on the need for a Nigerian nation with all relevant partners and stakeholders agreeing to stay together. If there was no document in 1914, a new one should be developed where the rights and privileges of federating units will be clearly specified and precisely stated. Also, the document will specify the roles and responsibilities of each federating unit and how one can, if desired, exit the federation.

Prior to the national constitutional conference, individual regions should meet, do their own constitutional conference, itemize what they want and do the national conference with their agreed memorandum to present and advocate for inclusion into the national constitution. Areas of agreement should be adopted immediately and areas of dissent should be further discussed at both national and regional levels before, based on equity, fairness and justice, the best options are accepted and implemented.

2. **Restructuring of Nigeria:** This may be one of the outcomes of the constitutional review and I see it as a major option for Nigeria. If this is agreed as the way forward, then, it should be implemented immediately. But, what must we restructure?

   a. *Restructure the Geography and Politics of Nationalism*. Although we have 527 ethnic groups in Nigeria, we cannot fragment into 527 regions. Rather, we should begin by returning to the former regional arrangement. The present six zonal system is very artificial and will not solve the problems we are facing. The old regional system (which by the way should still be in operation as the 1963 Constitution is the only democratically developed constitution in Nigeria) is the best way to restructure with immediate public acceptance. With regional restructuring, the centre shall be made less attractive but still very vital. Each region should be allowed to develop at its own speed – have its own revenue management system, police and civil service. The federal should just coordinate international relationships and forestall international aggression. We can replicate the United Arab Emirate Model as much as possible.

b. ***Restructure Resource Management Systems:*** Every region should be responsible and accountable for resources in their region, and pay an approved percentage of the gross earnings to the federal government. This will allow regions to be creative and innovative in resource development and management, rather than wait on the federal government's monthly hand-outs. Empowered regions will feed funds into the federal government on monthly or quarterly basis. Regions will become economic superpower for a rebranded Nigeria.

c. ***Restructure Federal Leadership System:*** Nigeria should have a ceremonial President with regional heads as Vice Presidents. Elections into the Office of the president should be within the Vice Presidents meetings with each Vice President serving as the President for a period of 24 calendar months. The President shall be empowered to head meetings of the Vice Presidents/Regional Heads and make relevant decisions in line with the mandate of the office. This will obviate the need for federal elections and the associated cost implications.

d. ***Restructure the National Assemblies and all National Structures:*** Few nominated individuals (about six per region) from the regions will populate National assemblies and other structures. For instance, the speakers and deputy speakers of each region will serve as compulsory members of national assemblies. Like the presidency, the leadership of the national assemblies shall be rotatory. No national leader should be allowed by constitution to lead for more than the 24 calendar months. However, if the person stays at the regional office long enough, they may lead again when it is the turn of their region. For equity and fairness, the appointment should respect the federating units' interest and spread.

e. ***Restructure Police and Defence Systems:*** We should completely restructure the police and defence systems with each region having its regional police that will complement the federal police. Defence will be purely a federal assignment; however, leadership of the different arms will be regionalized with all regions effectively represented in any federal Security Council meeting. Just as federal and national assemblies' leadership are rotatory, leadership of the various arms of the defence system shall also be rotatory respecting the federating units to ensure fairness and equity in the administration of the system.

f. ***Rework the Arms and Ammunition Policies:*** People should be licenced to carry arms for self-defence. If widely implemented, kidnapping and armed robbery will be reduced significantly. However, all purchases should be from regional police for proper control and documentation of arms in circulation. Procurement should also follow proper psychological assessment and only to individuals with a known and regular means of income, tax clearance and social/life insurance.

g. ***Reorganize the Systems and Processes:*** Both federal and regional governments should work to put processes in place that respect the new governance structure. This will include financial, demographic, and informational processes that will limit crime, improve documentation, and ensure excellent feedback systems. For instance, everybody within the regions should have a unique identification number; every street (including rural paths) should be properly surveyed, demarcated and named, and every house should have a street number and address. Naming systems should be standardized (e.g. First Name, Middle Name or Initials and last/surname) Vehicle licenses, bank accounts, and unique IDs of people should be linked to their numbered houses; and a central data system should triangulate all information into one single page. This will help all aspects of governance and improve revenue generation.

h. ***Return of Oil Wells:*** All oil wells in this nation should be as matter of urgency be returned to the government. Moving forward, each state should own and operate the oil wells in them, and pay a percentage commission to the federal government. States should operate these wells and use the resources to pay their bills including salaries and wages, pension, and infrastructural development. For states that have too many oil wells, some can be leased to neighbouring states (and as a last resort, the federal government) at a cost to help them meet their financial obligations. On no account should individuals own oil wells again in Nigeria. However, if individuals must own and run the oil wells, majority should come from the oil rich regions who are supported with resources from the government to acquire and operationalize the wells.

i. ***Restructuring of the Foreign Exchange and Cabals.*** These are major challenges of Nigeria and if not resolved may sink the Nigerian ship. People with import license collect foreign currencies at no cost from the Central Bank and exchange same at the parallel market within hours to make humongous incomes. This must be restructured. What qualifies an organization as an importer and exporter, what qualifies an individual as an importer and exporter must be properly specified. And true importers and exporters must be equitably spread across the nation. Bureau de Change business must be restructured and all parts of Nigeria given licences to operate as against a single locality currently being practiced.

These are the basic things I believe we can do as quickly as possible. Let the race to rescue Nigeria by rebuilding the foundations begin in earnest through constitutional review that will approve this restructuring process. Further delay may cause more harm than can be imagined. Any individual, group or tribe that refuses these suggestions is/are among those benefiting erroneously from the current unhealthy structure and chaotic systems

If the truth most be told, and I must say it, we have lost everything we held dear in Nigeria – peace, friendship, security and love for the nation. It is time to rebuild the nation and ensure that the vision of our founding fathers and the dreams of our children are not jettisoned. We all must do this together. Every enemy of the state should be revealed and punished.

Leaders should begin to respect the rule of law and our reworked constitution. Every tribe, religion and peoples should be law abiding. Total and holistic restructuring must begin with us.

In a public function recently, a notable Vice Chancellor said, "All Nigerians are good people, but the things we do make our nation bad". Also, a former Senate President shared on the Concept of Shame (which is lacking in Nigeria), Issue of corruption (which is rampant at all levels of the nation), and the Concept of guilt (which majority of evil doers in Nigeria do not have) during a book presentation. It is time to clean up Nigeria of these labels. Everyone has a role to play.

3. **Economic Strategic Plans:** No nation succeeds without a plan as failure to plan is planning to fail. Nigeria has tried to plan a number to times without actually completing the process. The latest was the Vision 2020. We are in the year 2020, but for over 10 years prior to this year, nobody has openly mentioned this Vision as a guide to Nigerians future.

Visions are critical to growth. Strategic plans are vital to the achievement of visions. With a restructured Nigeria, there is the need to develop new visions and plans for the future we want to see. For instance, can we be a developed nation in a third world continent?

This is very possible as South Africa has already achieved this long ago. Can we move from a consumer nation to a producer nation? Yes, as we are already blessed with so many natural resources including crude oil, and we gain nothing by exporting raw materials when we can use them to create millions of jobs for the jobless youths to turn them into finished products that will bring in amazing foreign exchange for the country. Just imagine the cost of crude and that of a computer or other finished products? We give our raw materials out for almost free and pay through our nose for the finished products. This should stop. To achieve our producer nation status, each region should focus on their area(s) of comparative advantages – agriculture, animal husbandry, solid minerals, crude oil exploration, etc. We should also dive into knowledge economy and set up industry hubs in all regions producing enough for the region and for exports. We should ensure adequate security and tax rebate to attract foreign companies to invest in the processes. We should have a plan to pay off the debts and make a vow not to borrow again – except it is expedient and must be approved by the people.

We must develop regional plans to rebuild the systems and structures (infra and human-structures) to ensure sustainable development and support systems for the development envisaged by the new national strategic plans. We must look at our people and empower them with world class skills and knowledge through a better educational system that must prioritize the health of our people by developing amazing first class hospitals, ensure universal access to healthcare services through a social insurance scheme and work with regions to ensure strong early child education, development of problems solving mentality and adequate insurance of life and property in case of untoward occurrences. The Economic strategic plan should feed into as well as be drawn from the national and regional long-term plans.

The economic strategic plan should also define when the different economic steps should be taken including return of all oil wells (immediately), review of import licences (within a quarter), review of foreign exchange guidelines (within six months), etc. Time and responsible individuals should be clearly spelt out.

Finally, we should move from speculative and spiritualizing everything to a knowledge based economy. Knowledge based economy will stimulate the use of best practices and innovative approaches for the development of creative products, businesses and processes that can create wealth and sustainable enterprises. In knowledge based economy, people use their heads and not their hearts to think. This is what we need in Nigeria. Beyond prayers and faith, we need a population of people that think, think and think to do what has never been done before across the world.

To ensure sustainable economic revolution, National/Regional business hubs should be created, planned an established in every region of Nigeria. These hubs shall serve as a platform for networking, marketing of products, establishment of contacts, and sales of Nigerian made products – cars, wares, electrical, drugs, perfumeries, etc. government will make the business hubs tax free zone to encourage investment, participation and excitement among young entrepreneurs. When completed, the business hub will be a one stop centre for all major high quality Nigerian products and services at reasonable prices.

4. **Long Term National and Regional Plans:** Beyond the economic strategic plans, every region should develop her long-term regional plans. This will have well developed segments

on economy, education, sports, health, technology, infrastructure, security, culture, tourism, agriculture, communication, religion, and socials. Each region can also add other sub segments that are unique to the regions.

The long-term plans should be for 20, 50 and even 100 years. These plans should have clear visions and milestones for each decade. Each regional long-term plan should be assembled to develop the national long-term plan. These long-term plans should be detailed enough to define the future we want but skeletal enough to allow for new developments and discovery in the future.

5. **Separation of Power:** One of the biggest challenges faced by the current system at all levels of governance is poor separation of power. The executive pays all the bills and therefore detects who does what and what happens at the legislative and judiciary. This is unhealthy and has led to several avoidable conflicts and bullying of the other arms of Government.

Moving forward, the reworked constitution and the restructured federation should accommodate proper and complete separation of powers between the three arms of government where none negatively influences the others directly or indirectly.

To achieve, this, the funding of each arm of government should come directly from an approved budget through the Central Bank. The nomination and appointments of officers in each arm should be completely devoid of executive influence or manipulations. The judiciary arm of government should be so independent that both executive and legislative are blinded to their decisions, judgements and activities. When this is achieved, each arm of government will serve as a check and balance to the rest bringing about healthy leadership and equity in governance.

6. **Educational Restructuring:** Education is the foundation of development and if Nigeria desires to be a first world nation, she must have a first world educational system. A nation where the best brains and those who can afford it have to go to other nations to study, learn and most times remain there is not a progressive nation. A nation where teaching at all levels are left for those who could not get better paying jobs or failed out of the systems/schools cannot be a great nation. A nation where education is not given priority in the national budget, nor funded through additional votes from the government cannot make global impact. Thus, the need for educational restructuring.

Nigeria, through the regions, must make teaching lucrative and attractive to the best brains. First class graduates should be seen from primary to university levels teaching, mentoring and life coaching our children. Students should have unhindered access to current books, electronic libraries, journals and bibliographies, and other reference materials. Students who are in technical classes should also have access to equipment and tools to practice their trade. Provisions should be made for industrial training, apprenticeship, and vocational trainings. Also, exchange programs should be encouraged across institutions, regions and national borders. Twinning programs and north-south partnerships should be fully supported.

As early child education is critical, only graduates – with Masters' Degree in early child development should be engaged to mentor and train children less than five years old.

Enough funds should be budgeted at the regional levels for educational activities and liveable wages paid to teachers to keep them motivated, engaged and involved in child education activities. Also, good income will improve the quality of teachers, and help attract the best brains to the classroom. School teachers and University professors should be enlisted to promote the need to teach among the best brains in the school so as to have the best and most qualified students choose teaching as their first career choice.

Finally, to enhance teaching, tools needed to teach must be provided, schools must be made conducive for learning, the environment must be made safe for both pupils and teachers and above all, regular review of curriculum must be done to keep the scheme of work alive and up to date.

Educational restructuring should also include close monitoring of what children are taught – whether in conventional schools or Islamic schools. Children should be protected from being brain washed with doctrines that will not lead to national development and prosperity. We should build a nation of knowledge-based economy not religion or emotional economy. We should empower children to become gods of their own not serve man made gods. We should turn our schools into research centres, productivity workshops and creative centres of excellence not just a system where children cram, pour and forget. We should train children to build their own machines, industries, vehicles, and make great discoveries. We should build a productive rather than a consumer society. We can make the changes we desire through the school we build, equip and manage.

Finally, we should establish centres of excellence across each region based on their comparative advantages, educational villages where creativity is key, special centres to do what no one has ever done and central libraries to provide good resources for research and development activities.

To support the educational evolutions, we should establish ICT hubs, industrial estates and demonstration farms. We should set up structures that will help our schools achieve their ultimate goals – changing the world for good for all.

7. **Power Initiative:** Electric power is critical to national development. Without power, small, medium and large scale industries cannot survive. People need to have access to electric power to be able to do simple day to day activities. To rebuild Nigeria, power sector must be fully decentralized, commercialized, and diversified.

Gas turbines, hydroelectric power systems, wind turbines, biofuels, solar energy and other natural sources of power must be developed and used to supply electric power to homes and offices. Massive investment by Government into electric power sector must be guided by a developmental plan and championed through public private sector initiatives. Regions should be allowed to develop their own power systems, and upload this into the national grid for financial returns. Solar farms should be established in communities that can manage them. Gas flaring should be banned and all gas channelled into electric power generation.

Children should be taught how to develop electric resources and new ways of generating power. Nigeria should start thinking of local content rather than importing everything and serving as a consumer nation. We should encourage creativity in this industry. Natural sources – air, water, biofuels, solar, etc. should be maximized extensively.

8. **Specialization and Core Competencies:** Every region should focus on their core area(s) with comparative advantage and develop it to become a world class expert in it. For instance, while the South-South may focus on oil exploration, refining and mass establishment of industries requiring oil and its produces as raw materials, the

South-East may focus on industrialization and development of *agriconomy* that maximizes the full value chain of the agricultural produce. In addition, they may also focus on small and medium scale industries turning Aba, Onitsha and Nnewi into major industrial hubs for vehicle and vehicle related products, drugs and chemicals, textiles and other related businesses. The South-West may decide to look into Cocoa production, and knowledge based economy with the establishment and management of multinational organizations. Similarly, the north should focus on solid mineral exploration and exploitation, animal husbandry and agriculture. With each region focusing on their core areas of competence, Nigeria will develop at the speed of light, there will be healthy competition and above all, jobs will be created, crime will be reduced as people are productively engaged and empowered.

To maximize regional specialization, there is the need for local initiatives that have global perspective. In addition, there is the need to adapt and localize technologies and developments towards having uniquely Nigerians technology. This was done in China, India, and several other nations of the world. Nigeria can, and should, work at doing the same. We need Nigerian Google, Yahoo,

Amazon, Bluehost, Facebook, etc. We need functional .ng and ng.gov sites. We need not just good presence in the net, but in a locally developed net system. We need truly Nigerian satellites in the sky, have Nigerians walk in the moon, have Nigerian car, phone, computer, bulb, etc. manufacturing – not assembling – companies. We need quality made in Nigeria goods for export. We need to see these goods in Nigeria, West Africa, Africa and global markets. We need to begin to build a Nigerian brand that makes sense across the nations of the world – and replace this with the current wrong image people have of Nigeria.

Nigeria need to be in charge of their destinies through functional technological advancement.

9. **Improved Border Securities and National Identification Number:** One of the biggest challenges Nigeria is facing resulting in insecurity is porous borders. Nigerian borders are open to all manner of people from all over the world. There are minimal checks at the borders with majority crossing through unmanned segments of the border. The absence of a verifiable National identification and numbering system makes it difficult to identify any non-Nigerian once they have

entered into the nation. But this can be corrected and modified. The borders can be sealed by a combined team of Immigration, Customs and National Defence Corps. As until the borders are sealed, criminals will not stop entering and criminalities and insecurity cannot stop. Also, the porous borders and absence of national numbers allow terrorists into Nigeria and their subsequent access to Nigerian International Passport – a deficiency that informed the recent USA banning on Nigerians who desire to immigrate into the United States.

The introduction of National Identification Numbers could be planned to ensure regional separation with special codes for each region. Individuals from each region will have numbers that are very unique and these numbers are linked to the individual's house, office, car, driver's license, international passport, bank BVN and even permanent voters card. A proper triangulation of all information will allow for people census, taxation and its returns and planning baselines.

With secure borders and national ID cards, Nigerians can be traced, identified and if missing, know where to find them. If this is coupled with a sensor device, it will also limit kidnapping and other evil works seen in Nigeria.

10. **National policies for growth and industrialization**. Policies and laws should be business friendly. Tax holidays should be maximized for investors. Visa on arrival should encourage tourism. We should remove the bureaucratic system that keeps people in the airport for over three hours before visa could be obtained and person allowed to proceed into Nigeria. Monetary and Fiscal policies will be modified to give people easy access to finances for investment and productivity.

Policies should be enacted that creates monetary communities, international tourist sites, etc.

Survey Report 3:
Solutions, Strategies and
Systems that Make Sense.

To the Questions, "What do you think are the three (3) best possible solutions for Nigeria out of these problems?", 314 solutions grouped into 39 classes were identified and mentioned. Restructuring and constitutional review, good leadership and government and citizens' education and reorientation topped the list as shown in Appendix 4.

Common solutions suggested include

Solutions	Percentage
Restructure Nigeria and Review Constitution	51
Install good leadership and inclusive government	44
Citizens education and orientation	28
Free and compulsory education	26
Strong and independent judiciary	15
Strong security including better welfare package for officers	14
Effective followership with responsibility	13
Adequate Job Opportunities	11
New Democratic Institutions with electronic voting system	10
Merit based systems	8
Better infrastructure including electricity	8

Improved infrastructures including IT, electricity and basic amenities	8

Some responses include;

"Overhaul our democratic institutions and fashioning out a 'democracy' that suites *(sic suits)* our level of development as a people."

"Treat Nigerians equal - no segregation. Appoint the right person on the job without sentiment."

"Set up a program in schools, instilling the love for country into the children from age 2."

"Create awareness of the danger of not responding to the wrong system of governance and administration in the hearts of every right citizen of this beloved country."

"Voting using an electronic system that cannot be compromised to avoid rigging thereby electing the people's mandate."
"Awarding any form of contract (social amenities and infrastructural amenities) to people of integrity."

"Cut down the outrageous allowance of Senators and House of Rep Members."

"The geopolitical zones should be removed and power at the centre should be reviewed. Political office holders should have a thorough reorientation on what it means to be a servant-leader."

"I suggest States to have their own security outfits, but with a Federal agency too. And our military training and recruitment should be based on merit not on sentiments/religious or zonal affiliations."

"Removing all the old leaders and their teams and electing new people with the aim to change Nigeria."

"Nigeria as a government should invest in IT related things. People who are interesting *(sic interested)* in IT fields like programming, communication and others struggle so much due to lack of a functional government policy guiding how telecommunication companies charge the users etc. if only Nigeria through Its agency can create a kind of competition for the telecommunication companies a lot will be improved."

"Complete overhaul of the educational system.... schools should work in sync with industries."

"Amendment of the 1999 constitution to ensure complete restructuring of the fiscal governance and political architecture in Nigeria. To start with, we can return to a modified 1963 constitution in which the Regions can be increased to 8 to provide adequately for the ethno-religious minorities in the North and the South."

"Death penalties should be introduced not just for politicians but anyone who acts in any manner that would favor a particular tribe or persons, every government process must."

"Definite wage structure based on dollar exchange rate to obtain dignity of labour and prevent worship of looters."

"An ALL-OUT National Reorientation Exercise aimed at Building Patriotism and Integration."

As the world is full of activities, we needed to know – due to limited resources – what solutions of the 40 groups the government should focus on. So, to the question, "Which problem should Nigerian Government focus as a priority?", 123 priority areas were mentioned which were classified into 22 groups as shown in Appendix 5. Government focusing on security, fighting corruption, and restructuring the nation were top on the list.

Top key focus areas are

Priority Area	Percentage
Security	32
Corruption	15
Restructure Nigeria	13
Leadership and Management	11
Unemployment	10
Education and Health	9
Infrastructural development	5
Economy	4

Meritocracy	3
Poverty	3

Some key comments by participants include,

"Corruption in its entirety at all levels, caucuses and groups."

"No leadership has genuine interest of Nigeria at heart so my advice will be wasted, let's separate."

"AUTHENTIC IDENTIFICATION OF ALL NATIONALS, FROM FAMILY, CLAN, TRIBE, REGION AND STATE. Not Religious Affiliations Qualifying People To Be Nigerians!!!"

"Information Technology. Let us create our own techniques of solving our own problems, let us stop employing the solutions provided by Europeans and Asians we are in an entirely different century with them."

"Insecurity should be addressed as a matter of urgency. Our porous borders must be secured to prevent the evil mercenaries from streaming in."

"Protection of the endangered Biafra's and Christians in general in Nigeria from the Muslim violence, killings and terrorism acts."

Pulse and Reflect:
Changing the Unhealthy Air Travel Environment

It is not unusual for a regular traveller in Nigeria to hear, "We are sorry for the delay in this air-flight. It was due to operational reasons." Anybody who has never heard this in Nigerian airports is yet to travel within Nigeria. This is what we hear day in day out in most Nigerian airports. Travelling to Owerri recently, my flight was delayed for two hours (12.05 to 14.05 hours) and we all received text messages to this effect. But even when we arrived at the airport, the plane did not take-off until an hour and a half later due to "operational reasons."

Coming back from Owerri, we were to leave the airport by 9.15 am, but again, this was not to be as we were later told that the operating plane will be arriving by 10.15 am from Lagos.

This has become the daily experience of most air travellers in Nigeria. Having your flight leave at the scheduled time now is a very rare occurrence in Nigeria. What a tragedy!

The impact of these on the economy of Nigeria, the psyche of people and the career of travellers are inestimable. Every delay negatively affects the individuals in the flight. Some miss their meetings.

Some miss their connecting flights. Some miss lifelong opportunities. Some even miss interview appointments and job offers. These happen on a regular basis because flights were delayed by the managements of the airlines.

To mitigate this, people now plan their trips a day earlier to avoid missing their international flights from Lagos, Port Harcourt or Abuja. This also has its associated cost – hotel, airport taxis, work not done, and time loss. Furthermore, these also expose travellers to several other social risk associated with hotel life, long absence from homes, and freedom in a strange environment.

The commonest reason for these delays is, "Operational reasons." I get sad anytime I hear this and wonder when we, as a people, will do something about it. Airlines should not be managed using "Operational Management Techniques", but as projects with clear tolerance limits and attention to time, quality and cost. Airlines are precise science and need management scientist who understand precise management techniques found in project management. At the various counters, checking in and bag management are still very time, energy, and human intensive, although many countries have automated these processes. In this trip to Owerri and from Owerri, the Boarding Pass printer was faulty (8.00 am), and people had to queue up for minutes just to check in. As if this was not enough, the

Boarding time was moved forward without informing the passengers. Also at the new boarding time, there was no evidence of the operating airline. One hour post the boarding time, passengers were still all seated and the flight was yet to arrive.

For a new and rebranded Nigeria, this MUST stop. Airline operators should understand the value of time and quality in their services. Speaking with a delayed customer, she said, "It is a product of our mentality. We have the wrong mentality over these issues." If this is the case (and I agree with her), airline operators' mentality should be reprogrammed and properly reoriented to understand the value of time and quality.

While preparing this article, I met the staff of one of the airlines who told me how life was made so difficult for their commuters. According to her, the airline sent a craft for routine services without adequate preparation for the commuters. Although they ended up refunding commuters their payments, these commuters had to pay higher fees to other airlines to make the same journey. Shouldn't this airline be sued for this? Is it not a best practice to plan ahead, and when this fails, to refund as well as give each client a free ticket for their next flight to assuage their losses, their time wasted and their anxieties?

Delays should be minimal. But this cannot be achieved if Nigerians fold their hands and expect somebody from another world or God to solve their problems. In all my international trips and trips within nations such as the United States, I have only suffered two delays and the reasons were clear. Even at that, the airlines gave all participants vouchers to either rebate next travel or buy inflight materials. Such gifts could not restore the time lost, but was sufficient to keep the airline on their toes as for every delay, they paid for it.

Unfortunately, this is not the case in Nigeria. There are no compensations for the delayed passengers. There are no punishments or losses to the operating airline. There is no restitution for the crimes of the airlines. Passengers are allowed to pay for the mistakes and inefficiency of the airline operators. For instance, passengers pay for extra nights they did not plan for, pay for airport taxis that was not in their initial itinerary, pay for rescheduling of flights that resulted from airline operators' delays and cancellations, miss their connecting flights and bear the consequences alone, and sometimes miss meetings, conferences and important life events like the birth of their new babies. All these are the burden of the customers. The airline loses nothing.

These anomalies are rampant in Nigeria and Nigeria alone. Why are things not working in Nigeria airline industry?

I have a few answers

1. **Because nobody cares.** People speak about the ills of the system, but nobody

really wants to do anything about it. People complain about the delays, the denials, and the disenchantment of the airline operators, but as usual, "It is not anybody's business." Thus, for so many years, we have lived under the oppressive leadership of the operators of these airlines. This should stop in the new Nigeria.

2. **Because delays and cancelations by airlines do not cost the airline operators anything.** They neither pay for the delays, cancelations, or the inconveniences. I was speaking to the air hostess on a flight, and her level of nonchalance was more disturbing. Imagine if the airlines were to give a 50% rebate to everyone whose flight was delayed in their next flight, and a free ticket for any customer whose flight was cancelled, there will be fewer delays and fewer flight cancellations.

3. **Because the regulating bodies and agencies are either ill-equipped for the job, ill-trained or compromised.** There is no evidence of a customer welfare agency or commission in these processes. "Nobody, even the government, cares" was the frustrated statement of a very angry customer whose flight was delayed for several hours on a different occasion.

4. **Because of customers' mentality of anything goes**. In Nigeria, customer rights are only stated in papers and never in reality. Customers' have, therefore, learned over the years to take anything without complaining, as they say, "Half bread is better than none." So when a flight is delayed, even if it is for hours, people still appreciate the airline for at least not cancelling the flight altogether. What a shame!

5. **Because of wrong religious mentality**. Nigerians are highly religious and very spiritual. This has made them believe that everything is of and from God – even the delays. They blame God for every of man's failures, man's inadequacies and man's shortcoming. This is a very wrong image of God, who said, "Be ye perfect, even as your heavenly father is perfect." A perfect God is not a time waster, but a trailblazer and a pathfinder. God does not break promises or covenants. God does not set up people to allow them to fail. God does not distort people's plans as He is a planner Himself. God believes in perfection, timeliness, order and in the use of patterns. God also commands followership and learning from those who have done better. Putting our inadequacies on God is, therefore, not fair. God is not to be blamed for our stupidity.

6. **The mentality of African/Nigerian time.** This is one major killer of development in Africa, especially in Nigeria where we have the Nigerian time in everything. We have come to believe and thus become non-timers. To a Nigerian, "Things can never happen according to plans." Even church services in some churches have to be put on hold until people arrive. Meetings have to wait until the big men arrive. Official programs have to wait until the top government officials arrive. If the government, who ought to be the watch dog of the society cannot keep to time, one is not, therefore, surprised that the agencies they supervise are not time conscious.

But can this change? YES. Nigeria can change. The airlines can do better at time management and service delivery. This is doable if there is a;

1. **Paradigm Shift in Management Principles:** Use of operational management approach is a mistake in the airline industry. This is a highly precise industry. They must move away from operational management to project management approach. With project management, the product is the asset of the organization. Projects are only successful when they are delivered to time, acceptable quality, and at an agreed cost. Use of project management is what is helping the rest of the world succeed. We must jump into this

best practice if a significant difference must be made.

2. **Training and Re-Training of all Staff:** While university education delivers certificates, good in-service trainings delivers capacity and skills. As sustainable development is human capital focused. All staff of the airline industry must be trained and retrained in project management, leadership and customer relationships if the desired changes must be achieved. The suggested training should take place in batches with the management team going first. Also, it should not be a one-off training, but a high competency based training with significant field component. The suggested trainings should be for a period of at least six months per batch with on the job mentoring, supervision and evaluation. Only staff that excel in these trainings should be retained in the industry.

Also, moving forward, all new staff should, apart from services oriented trainings and inductions, be exposed to significant project management even before their first day on their duty post. This will give them the needed push to make a difference. These trainings should bring about change, reemphasize on core values and codes of conducts, develop airline creeds and continuously make the needed changes that the airline industry need. Airline operators must use the best trainers to get the best.

3. **Mass Action against the Airlines:** Another thing that may quickly trigger changes and better commitment to the care and welfare of the clients is a national mass action against the airlines. Such an action will shake them and galvanize them into doing the right things all the time. A mass action that will cost the airline billions to trillions of Naira will definitely send the right message. I look forward to a changed airline industry that meets the needs of the new Nigeria of our dreams.

Chapter 5

Change Begins with Me (#CBWM)

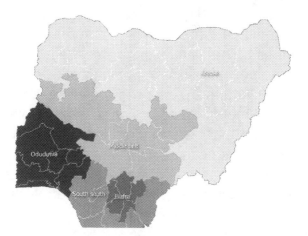

I am tired of the state of Nigeria. We were promised change. Yes, there have been a number of changes – people are dying of hunger, the economy is in recession, students cannot pay their school fees, salaries of workers are not paid (and when paid, only part of their dues are paid), no new roads are being constructed, the electricity generation has gone down, companies are closing and leaving Nigeria, people are losing their jobs, people cannot pay their hospital bills, public offices are becoming more and more inefficient and politicians are playing with the destinies and lives of the electorate. Yes, there have been a number of changes; but is this the change Nigerians expected?

I like the slogan – **Change Begins with Me** (#CBWM) – even though I do not really like the inherent hypocrisy.

At the airport in Nigeria, I saw a highly placed civil servant with a Federal Ministry drop his waste on the ground. The first thing that occurred to me was, "Change Begins with Me". For the first time, I voiced it, he looked at me, picked up the paper, and a few moments later, told me to correct with civility. This showed me that becoming an ambassador for the #CBMW mantra can actually bring positive changes within our nation. I agree that change is needed and change must begin with me. I have, therefore, decided to be part of the mobilizers for this change and thus the essence of this Pulse and Reflect – change.

In US, I was challenged by the fact that things were different there. Things are different, not because the people are saints, but because they have functional systems. Things are different not because they are perfect in any way (far from it), but because the system encourages innovation, creativity, entrepreneurship and out of the box mentality. They are different because they believe in themselves, believe that

America is the greatest and does NOT depend on anybody or any nation for anything. They are different because they are almost 100% self-sufficient and only use other nations of the world to advance their agenda. They are different because they have taken (for over 200 years) the full responsibility for their national development and advancement.

Nigeria can and should also change. Change is, we are told, the only constant thing in life. However, change could be positive or negative. Change can be natural or man-made. Change can be progressive or retrogressive. And change can be planned or unplanned. I have said over the past seven years that all natural changes are primarily negative. Yes, negative, because the world is programmed to operate in random motions. We grow by eating and taking care of ourselves. If we allow nature to guide our lives, we will die from malnutrition (natural change). We clean our environments to avoid diseases. If we don't, the environment will become a threat to live and healthiness. Just take a moment and think about all the natural changes you can remember – they are all negative. Even aging is negative – bringing you closer to your grave and chronic diseases.

True, progressive, positive and sustainable changes are man-made, man-initiated, man-triggered, man-implemented and man-powered. And for Nigeria to become better, the changes that we desire in economy, politics, security, education, health, environment, policies, community and family live must begin with us. With a population of over 180 million people, if each of us chooses to change, chooses to add value to Nigeria every single day, chooses to be positive and not negative, chooses to be a blessing to our nation, chooses to make meaningful contribution to the economy, society and politics, Nigeria will in less than 50 years from now be a world super power. Change, truly begins with us.

But, in as much as this is true, do we believe in this? Do we truly want the kind of change that will move Nigeria forward? If we do, then this will be a welcomed guide to help us make the right decisions, take the right steps and ensure the right kind of developments and improvements in Nigeria. However, if we don't, it will be a reason for our annoyance and maybe desire to fight using the instruments of government.

I agree that Change Begins with Me. It also begins with the President, his cabinet, the National Assembly, the Ministers, the Judiciary and the Governors. We must change and focus on the key priorities like corruption, and fight it in a way that must be seen to be just, fair and free. Focusing on corruption as an entity is both myopic and unproductive. We must fight corruption by building sustainable systems that make sense. We must generate enough electricity to run the systems. We must automate whatever can be automated and keep within reach of the people information that will help them make meaningful contribution to national development.

Change must begin with us – a case of leadership by example. We must change in the process of selection and appointment of officers to rule Nigeria. During one of my trips to New York, I met a Nigerian who knew one of the very important Ministers. His disappointment on her appointment was very obvious. In his words, "She knows nothing. We teach her what to say when she comes here." What a tragedy. We have a lot of square pegs in round holes. We should change by changing present cabinet members, government processes and priorities.

Change must begin with us – we must change Nigeria by bringing back all our girls, ending the insurgence of militants, Boko Haram and kidnappers. We must respond to national issues rather than reacting to them. We must work to make Nigeria great again.

Nigerian government, entrepreneurs and businessmen must allow change to begin with them as they change Nigerian dependency on foreign donors and development partners, and foreign goods. We must change our belief systems and begin to appreciate who we are and what we have. We have believed several lies for so long that the time has come for a new way of thinking. 99% of what we see in America are made in America. 90% of what we see in Britain are made in Britain, but less than 1% of what we see in Nigeria are made in Nigeria – not even in the Federal Ministries or National Orientation Agency. We must look inwards, we must support local businessmen, we must support researches to develop Nigeria, and we must build Nigeria up from the scratch. Partners and foreign goods cannot make Nigeria great. We must change our belief systems and appreciate who we are and what we have. The time has come for a new way of thinking and reasoning.

True change in Nigeria requires that Nigeria change her economic dependency on oil, stop exporting raw materials (including crude oil) that could be transformed into finished products in Nigeria, stop importing any and everything into Nigeria – even from sister third world nations. We must change our economic polices (if we have one) and make them people oriented. Where none exist, we must craft policies that will change Nigeria from a consumer nation to a productive nation. We must support local manufacturing, local production, and development of local competence and capacities.

Nigeria must change her attitude to work and public assignments. Change begins with us. Public servants in airports and everywhere must change and stop the begging and bribing syndrome. We must take our work serious and be measured not on how long we worked, but how productive we were. Nigerians must change on their management of waste – waste should be disposed in ways that make sense (sorted and recycled). We should dispose waste in healthy manners, wash hands as frequently as is possible, and ensure that every home has toilets and waste disposal systems. We can begin this with proper waste segregation in all public and private offices across Nigeria, support waste to wealth technology, and use this to create thousands of self-sustaining jobs for hungry Nigerians.

Press must change their hypocritical reporting of government strengths and silence on government weaknesses. Asking for brown envelops before issues are published should stop as this biases reports and ensures that only what is paid for is seen – and as expected, in ways and manners that pleases the payers.

We should design, develop, implement and operationalize systems that will reduce corruption, ensure adequate tracking of funds, and monitoring of government expenses. The national population commission should change as it vows to give Nigeria a population figures that is devoid of falsifications and lies. The National Health Insurance Scheme (NHIS) should change by using available funds to give healthcare access to Nigerians rather than buying new houses for operators. The National Primary Health Care Development Agency (NPHCDA) should change as it makes primary healthcare services available to Nigerians rather than using available funds to travel and hold conferences that do not add value to health and the healthcare system. The aviation industry should change as they give Nigerians and her people value for money in timeliness and quality of services rather than hiding their shame in "delays due to operational reasons". The healthcare operators should change as they begin to ensure quality of care and promotion of well-being of Nigerians rather than multiple self-promoting strikes and deliberate undermining of the healthcare system. Yes, change begins with me. It begins with us.

Mahatma Gandhi emphasized this when he said, **"Be the change you want to see."**

Can we all be the change we want to see? Can we stop hunting people and face national development? Can we start by electing and/or appointing qualified Nigerians to run the affairs of the nation? We should change by focusing on national development rather than self-promoting programs and trips?

Will the National Assembly change by minimizing all forms of corruption, budget padding, bribery for approval of MDA budgets and use of constituent funds to build personal empires? Will the judiciary change as they give unbiased and just judgments to Nigerians? Will the governors and their allies within the states change as they build sustainable projects and pay workers their salaries as and when due? Will the civil servants change as they work at least 8 hours per day, treat every file without waiting for any form of bribe and "motivation" from service seeking Nigerians?

Yes, change begins with me (#CBWM). What about you. Beyond conferences, seminars and workshops, scientist must change and do researches that will improve the communities. We must change from dependency on foreigners to use of local resources to develop Nigeria.

Change begins with change in our utterances – rather than chasing away investors with our comments, we should be attracting investors with positive comments and branding; change economic policies to make businesses profitable, change employment policies to open up new opportunities

We must change. We all can partner with true government to become ambassadors of change as we change our ways and do what is right. Yes, Change Begins with Me.

Pulse and Think:
The Labour Union Issue in
Nigeria: A time to Rethink

One thing that has rubbished Nigeria is labour union strike actions. A labour union is an organization of workers that bargains with management on its members' behalf and usually unions represent their members in negotiations for wages, working conditions, fringe benefits, rules relating to seniority, layoffs and firings, and other matters[1]. There are two categories of labour union - Craft union membership which is made up of workers who have specific skills (such as medical doctors), and industrial union which represents all workers in a specific industry, e.g. workers performing different jobs in the health sector may be represented by the Joint Health Workers Association (JHWA).

In Nigeria, the Nigerian Labour Congress was founded in 1978 as an amalgamation of four rivalry centres - Nigeria Trade Union Congress (NTUC), Labour Unity Front (LUF), United Labour Congress (ULC) and Nigeria Workers Council (NWC). The unions, numbering over 1,000 were also restructured into 42 industrial unions[2]. According to Mike Alogba

---

[1] Welch, Patrick J. *Economics: Theory and Practice, 10th Edition*. John Wiley & Sons, 11/2012. Pg 445

[2] http://en.wikipedia.org/wiki/Nigeria_Labour_Congress

Olukoya[3], "the (NLC) was established to propagate and protect both specific and general interests of the Nigerian worker; be it white, blue or other colours of collar… It is estimated that there are more than 4 million workers belonging to the NLC.

While labour union activities are on the increase in Nigeria, they are on the decrease in advanced nations. For instance, in USA, in 1983, 20.1% of all wage and salary employees belonged to unions, but since then membership has fallen. By 2011, only 11.8 percent of their workers were unionized with a majority of these from the public sector (37% of government workers as against 6.9% of private sector workers).

Most Union and management negotiations are primarily about economic issues: wages, job security, payments for insurance, and such. Negotiation involves a give-and-take process where each side tries to gain the most of what it seeks while giving up the least. However, this has reduced significantly in advance counties as the erosion of union membership and power in USA stemmed from many sources: an antiunion political climate; growth in service sector jobs; the decline in blue-collar manufacturing jobs; expanded government regulation of working conditions; and retirements of union workers who were strong advocates for the union movement.

---

[3] Olukoya, M. A. (2010, May 1). NLC to Reward Employers. *NLC 2010 Employers Awards* . Lagos.

The key effect of labour unions across the world is strikes (or industrial actions/unrest) against the employer resulting from failure of the parties to a negotiation to agree on the terms of a contract. The purpose of the strike is to bring economic pressure on the employer to return to the bargaining table and draft an agreement acceptable to the union. In recent years in USA, little labour time has been lost due to strikes - less than 0.005 percent of estimated working time was lost because of work stoppages in 2010[4].

However, the Nigerian experience is the exact opposite. How much is Nigeria losing from the various strikes on daily basis. How many lives are lost and will be lost in the various doctors' strikes? I was told of a doctor who said, "it is better to lose few lives today, than to lose many more tomorrow" following a discussion on the recent doctor's strike in Nigeria. Can Nigeria ever migrate to an advanced world with the current labour practices, work cultures, and workers' attitudes to work?

I hear people daily comparing Nigeria with other developed world. But my question is, what are we doing as individuals to make Nigeria look like the developed world? The developed world did not fall from heaven. They were made by men and

---

[4] U.S. Bureau of the Census, Statistical Abstract of the United States: 2012, 131st ed., p. 428

women like us. We run to them to seek solace from challenges. We use them as mirrors to identify what is not working in Nigeria. But what exactly in concrete terms are we doing to change the state of Nigeria and make Nigeria compete with other global economies like the new Asian tigers.

Wise men ride on the shoulders of those who have gone ahead of them to see clearer. I think we should learn from the developed nations – not just by importing their foods and finished products to Nigeria, but more importantly by importing their best practices and skills which will help us shift from a dependent nation to a truly independent nation.

As long as we keep practicing what other nations have left behind centuries ago, we will remain in their past and never be able to compete favourably or as equals.

Moving forward, labour unions should be deemphasized, legally reengineered and politically erased *(I am sure many will want to kill me for saying this)*. This will help build a new crop of workers with better productivity mentality able to add values to the industrial world of Nigeria. Correct me if I am wrong, majority of our challenges is NOT government – after all, the current officers in government were a few months ago also going on strike as workers to drive home their demands. Our problem is ourselves!

We must make the decisions. The harder the decision, the greater the outcome. As our decisions determine our destination, our desire to be an industrialized nation must begin with the right decisions and legislations. No one can do everything, but everyone can do something meaningful. Begin from where you are today. Remember, Change Begins with Me.

Chapter 6

Building a Nation that Makes Sense: The Need for a Unique Identity for Each Nigerian

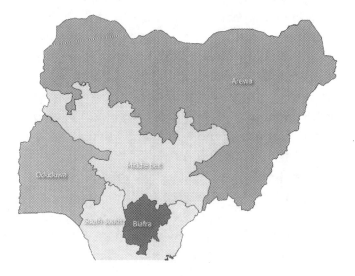

Chaos in the system makes the system bad and ineffective/inefficient. A few may profit from it, but the masses will always suffer. It is amazing that Nigeria, as rich and prominent as she is, has made little or no progress since 1960 when she peacefully obtained her independence from the British. Before you say I am wrong, please hear me out. We have governed ourselves for 60 years, fought a war in which there was neither a victor nor a vanquished, allowed ourselves to be derailed by policies that institutionalize mediocrity and dependency, and lived primarily as a consumer nation exporting raw materials rather than an exporter of finished products.

Despite being the 'largest economy in Africa' all human development indices are negative as Nigeria is said to have some of the worst health indicators globally – life expectancy, under-5 mortality rate, maternal mortality ratio, disease burdens (malaria, polio and HIV), road traffic injuries, gender abuse, etc. Also unemployment rate, school drop outs rates, fake drugs, and several social vices are all on the increase. Today we have the GSM but we have lost or losing most native languages. Today we have better roads but more road traffic deaths and injuries. Today we have better houses, but majority of Nigerians are homeless and helpless. Today we have more universities, but less skills and capacities. We also have more banks, airlines, networks and hotels, but less real services to Nigerians. Nigeria can and should do better!

One wonders therefore why we have not made any meaningful difference in the lives of Nigerians despites several constitution review meetings, sovereign national conferences, town hall meetings, and campaign manifestos.

I have been thinking. For instance, since the early 19th century, malaria has been and has remained a major cause of death and hospital attendance in Nigeria. There have been more than 10 national malaria control strategies with similar objectives – to half the incidence of malaria by 50%, and with these strategies billions of Naira have been spent on malaria control strategies. However, the disease still remains a major cause of death, loss of man hours, and handicap of persons, especially the under-5 and pregnant women. Why?

I have come to believe that is it difficult to plan for a people that we cannot see, nor for a population that we do not know. For instance, who is a Nigerian? Do we truly know how many we are in this country? How many persons carrying a current Nigerian passport are truly Nigerians? How many schools do we need to meet the educational needs of Nigerian children at all levels? How many health workers do we need to produce to meet the global acceptable standards? How many new housing projects will be able to provide enough accommodation for the homeless Nigerians? How many new jobs do we need to create annually to mitigate unemployment? How many new cities do we need to build to prevent the emergence of new slums in the next 20, 50 or 100 years? How much food do we need to produce to prevent hunger, avoid famine and ensure food security?

For 60 years, we have merely *guesstimated* (not even estimated) our population, our needs, and our successes. Our census figures are all fraud. Our INEC voting list are either incomplete or full of ghost voters. Our birth registration service is limited and incomplete. The sad thing is that no one truly cares.

How can you plan for a people you do not know? I think it is time for us to go back to the very foundation of planning – counting and counting accurately. We can triangulate available data from various units in the Ministries of International Affairs, Health, Finance and Education, but this will not give us good data for futuristic plans. We need to count ourselves.

This we can do by simply giving every Nigerian a UNIQUE identity number – call it National security number, or national ID number or whatever; but every Nigerians need an identity card with traceable number. The technology for this is already in place. We only need to pay for it and adapt it to meet our needs.

As all previous national ID projects were programmed to fail from the very beginning, if we MUST succeed, we must change the way we do things. We must use the right skills and competences, we must allow the process to evolve through a proper structured pattern and we must make the process self-funding and self-sustaining. This we can start and conclude within 24 months and thereafter update the list with birth and death registration and certificates, in-migration and ex-migration of registered Nigerians as well as other national data systems.

To start this process, we need to identify the right skill sets. For once, let us bury nepotism and quota system and move Nigeria forward. It is not impossible to know who a Nigerian is. It is not impossible to have a street address in every nook and cranny of Nigeria leading to traceable addresses for all Nigerians. It is not impossible to have functional postal codes for every address in Nigeria making tracking simpler. It is NOT impossible. Doing this will not only make Nigeria a better nation and create hundreds of thousands of reliable and self-sustaining jobs, but will also generate real data for planning and decision making.

Nigeria has been chaotic for too long. The time has come for us to begin to put shape and structures in place. We must begin to take responsibility for a new Nigeria. This does not require rocket science as the technology is already in existence, has been tried in several other nations with excellent results and can easily be adapted and domesticated to make Nigeria project work. But do we have the WILL? To build a new Nigeria, we need to know who we are, how many we are and where we are. Let the counting begin now.

Pulse and Reflect:
Freeing Nigeria from the PAST

"Change is the law of life and those who look only to the past or present are certain to miss the future." - John F. Kennedy.

This is because the longer you live in the past, the less of the present and the future you have to enjoy. No nation is defined by their past – the past effectively prepares us for the future as we maximize the present.

I have lived in this nation long enough to know that no matter how long we blame our founding fathers, our colonial masters, the civil war, our parents or uncles for what we think they should have done but failed to do, what we think they did wrongly or what we think they ought not to have done, these will NEVER create the future that Nigeria or Nigerians deserve.

We must therefore put the past behind us. We must accept that we have moved beyond it as no matter how bad the past was, we can always begin again. Colonial era is over. Military rule is over. Biafra war is over. Aba women's riot is over. Ali must go is over, etc. If they are over, we must let them pass as holding unto the past will make us pass with the past.

Today, we have democracy, we have civilian rule led by a civilian president, we have internet, we have GSM, we have public and private educational facilities, we have oil, we have a constitution, we have policies and Acts, we have graduates and professors, we have farmers and entrepreneurs, we have great weather and wonderful climate. The list is endless. We have a lot, but still our eyes have always remained at the past. What a travesty of destiny.

Let us move on. In life, we understand that the best way to predict the future is to invent it. To invent the future, we have the responsibility to work on ourselves and our friends to build a greater fruitful and more fulfilling future. We should build on the three tiers of government to create the democracy that we need. We need to reinvent the culture of values that will give our children and grandchildren the future they deserve. We need to maximize our resources to build an economy that makes sense – not just the largest economy in Africa, but an economy that puts resources in the hands of the masses thereby reducing the level of poverty while empowering people to live healthier lives.

We need to respect and implement the acceptable reviewed Constitution of Nigeria, the policies and Acts establishing the various organs of government and ensure that nobody lives above the law. We need to use our resources – graduates and professors - to develop and invent new and better ways of living thereby transforming Nigeria into an industrialized nation. We need to use the internet and GSM to develop a culture of free communication and sharing of resources and information for the advancement of the nation and annihilation of wickedness and all evils in the land.

We need to transform Nigeria from a country that exports raw materials to one that exports finished products. We need to reduce our expenditure in importation as we build functional industries through the establishment of constant power supply. We need to empower our farmers to feed Nigerians and entrepreneurs to build sustainable businesses. We need to appreciate God for the excellent weather and ensure we do not destroy the ecosystem through unhealthy habits and uncontrolled development. We must guard against self-destruction as we censor advertisements and wrongful westernization of the country.

We must replace evil with good, laziness with diligence and mediocrity with excellence. We MUST move from operational management approach in life and governance to project management with well-defined timelines, quality criteria and cost implications.

We can make it happen. We can all start now. The FUTURE of NIGERIA is HERE. Let us all make it a reality.

Chapter 7

Heralding United Nations of Nigeria (UNON)

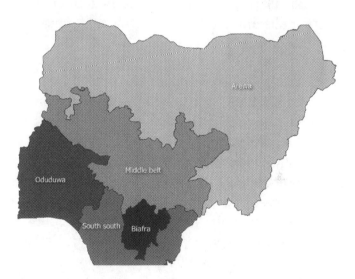

The global discontentment in the Nigerian nation is getting out of hand and restructuring mentioned by over 50% of the respondents as the way forward. Let me end the book my making some suggestions in this regard.

The north is angry, the south is angry. The middle belt, Niger Delta, and the Igbos are all angry. People are dying because of this anger, hate speeches and private group agenda are seen everywhere. Today, people are no longer safe in their homes and towns. Farmlands are not safe for farmers and crops are not safe from cattle and goats. Seas are not safe for fishermen, roads are not safe for travellers and neighbours are no longer friends. Villagers, politicians, public servants, police and the army have all fallen to the bullet of enemies of the nation. Everyone is afraid and on the watch. No one knows who the next victim would be.

In addition, the nation is not developing. The economy is crumbling. Diseases (like Lassa fever, Coronavirus (COVID-19), HIV, Tuberculosis, Malaria, etc.) are killing people in different parts of the nation and everybody – including the government – stands aloof watching. States cannot pay salaries. Government debt is increasing as government is still borrowing! Leaders are not transparent or accountable. Parastatals and agencies are collapsing. Mediocrity is institutionalized, and religion and ethnicity are being used as weapons of national destruction. Most people sit, watching, while others are uninterested. This is unacceptable in a nation like Nigeria.

Many have therefore questioned the current Nigerian structure. Many more are wondering – is Nigeria still a viable nation? The killings and devastations are current issues of public health hazards resulting in mass burials and epidemic of diseases, hence the need for this alert – **Heralding United Nations of Nigeria UNON)**.

That the current architecture and structure of Nigeria is not working is a known fact; the terrible mistake of amalgamation of Nigeria in 1914 by Lord Lugard and the desire of every tribe and language in Nigeria for a better Nigeria is common knowledge; and not restructuring Nigeria will be the worst disservice any leader will do to Nigeria. Restructuring has become an indisputable reality.

Today, several voices across the world are asking for restructuring. Many have died while several are imprisoned for this cause. Interestingly, none has said what the new Nigeria should look like.

Let me begin by saying that we can remain as one Nigeria – but there is an URGENT need for internal rearrangement – in policies, programs, and management styles.

Some people have called for total separation. This sounds logical going by the degree of nepotism, injustice, and inequality in the geographical location called Nigeria – but this may not be the best option as the world is coalescing into a small village resulting in large companies and nations consolidating rather than separating. Others have called for return to the regional system of government that existed before the

Biafra war. This may be seen as retrogressive – even though it may be a necessary step forward. We need a completely new arrangement that will favour the majority while at the same time delivering the desires of the people which is a progressive Nigeria. Thus, the need for **United Nations of Nigeria (UNON).**

A properly planned UNON will put into consideration the various needs of the people and the different nationalities in the current Nigeria and grant each their desired autonomy. Currently, we have the following major nationalities – Arewa, Oduduwa, Niger Delta, Middle Belt and Biafra. These five nationalities will in the new arrangement constitute the new Nigeria nations. The geographical space occupied by any of these are already known but can be finalized in a regional conference or referendum to decide who stays where and with whom. People and communities should be given the freedom to decide where they want to belong. Moreover, the terms of relationship (may and should) vary from nation to nation. This should be captured in the various national constitutions to be developed and adopted by each nationally.

A United Nations of Nigeria (UNON) will have a Union Leader – a President drawn from one of the five nations. This position will be rotational on a two-yearly basis. There will be no general election for this position as the next president will be selected from the Leaders of the various Nations. The leaders of the remaining four nations will serve as Vice Presidents. The President and the four VPs will constitute the Union Executive Council (UEC). There will be no need for a Union parliament, but a Union Supreme Court will be constituted to handle Union related issues and dissolved when all the critical Union issues are resolved. An ad-hoc Court may be constituted subsequently at the instance of the Union Executive Council (UEC).

Each nationality will have a National Leader – with a title as determined by the respective nations. There will also be a single national parliament, judiciary, and civil service in each nation. Each nation will have their Ministers, Ambassadors and embassies across the nations of the world, National embassies can co-exist in the same location by choice. Each nation can run a state or region-based system as they choose. Funding of Nations shall be based on revenues internally generated and natural resources within the nation. Each nation will be required to remit five (5) percent of their national income to the Union for Union development and governance.

The new Union will be guided by the word "UNION" as defined below,

1. **United Association**. It will be a unitedly-loose association of five different nationalities (Arewa, Oduduwa, Niger Delta, Middle Belt and Biafra) with unique systems of governance, technology, socialization, and economy.

Each member nation will develop her own infrastructures, systems and structures; but still make a meaningful contribution to the Union development – international roads, rails and security.

2. **Nationalities.** Each nationality will be responsible for national security, social amenities, internal and international policies, etc. Each nationality will have independent systems and structures that are not linked to any other nationality. Although they are independent, movement from one nation to the next will be free and without the need for a visa. Nationalities of any nation in the group are free to have structures, businesses, and systems operational in any nation of their choice – but within the laws of that independent country.

3. **Independent System**. Independent structures, judiciary, executive and legislative will be encouraged. There will be a few things that the nations will do together like having a Union President. Each nation will have an independent economy, electoral processes, police, etc. And will grow economically and technologically at their own pace.

4. **Oneness**. Although they are five different nationalities, they will be one in some unique ways like one Union President, One Union

Language, Union Security system and One Union Currency. Annual Union meetings will help ensure symbiotic relationships. Although there will be four Vice Presidents, each will have a unique portfolio covering National Collaborations and Partnerships, Technology and International Development, Economy and Finance, and Union Vision.

5. **Networking**. The nationalities will network with each other in a symbiotic manner to support their internal cohesion and growth. There will be such policies as UNON first – meaning importation from sister nation, use of sister nation material and products, involvement of sister nation in business deals, etc. This way, each nation will support the rest to grow and develop as quickly as possible.

The development and institutionalization of UNON will herald an end to most of the current challenges that the present Nigeria is facing.

Let's all be part of UNON and give it the support it needs. *A United Nations of Nigeria (UNON) is the simple, single and sustainable solution that Nigeria needs.*

God bless United Nations of Nigeria (UNON). Let's together make it happen. This is the New Nigeria we need.

Chapter 8

The COVID-19: Comprehensive Containment Strategy

As I was about finalizing this book for publication, the entire world was hit by Coronavirus (COVID-19) pandemic. This led to several public health directives including stay at home, frequent handwashing, social distancing, self-isolation, quarantine of travellers, and use of chloroquine. In addition, there were daily updates from World Health Organization, Nigerian Center for Disease Control, responses from national and state governments, public and private sector involvement, and massive social media campaigns.

Nigerian government established various committees under the leadership of the NCDC, developed manuals and guidelines, and used highly sensitive testing algorithms. Cases were managed either in government tertiary health facilities or make shift centers like in Lagos.

With over 859,032 (121.91/1,000,000 people) confirmed cases as at April 1st 2020, 178,101 recovered and 42,322 deaths; there is the need to take proactive steps to prevent the high rate of morbidity and mortality associated with pandemic in the future. In Nigeria, with 139 confirmed cases and two deaths, the epidemic is just beginning.

I recommend a deliberate proactive leadership approach for outbreak management. Deliberate proactive (DP) leaders think ahead, plan ahead, prepare ahead, and communicate deliberately and proactively. They are not prophets of doom, but are both realistic and futuristic. To manage the current epidemic and prepare for future ones, Nigerian leaders must;

Think Ahead: Please note that there will be more epidemics and pandemics in the coming years. The major enemies of the world are not the nuclear weapons of USA, China, North Korea, Russia, Iran, etc.; but the biological weapons of nature and man. Man will fight more battles with both emerging and re-emerging diseases. The world should know and plan for them. Current immunity, drugs, and vaccines will not be able to prevent this. Nigeria should plan for this. Establishing NCDC was a great deliberate proactive step. Empowering and reengineering NCDC to handle these proposed challenges must start now.

Plan Ahead: Nigeria must put plans in place to make quicker diagnosis of new infections, develop quicker vaccines, drugs and build herd immunity irrespective of the nature and cause of the epidemic. This is the only way the devastating effects of the coming epidemics will be prevented and avoided. Thus modalities must be put in place for accelerated institutional review board approval for study protocols, equipment and consumables for the production of drugs, vaccines, and diagnostics for future outbreaks, We should also have stand by team who will investigate and control the epidemic though early diagnosis, accelerate case management, and effective contact tracing.

Prepare Ahead: The high level of mortality and morbidity associated with COVID-19 was ascribed to lack of preparation by national government and responsible institutions. Nigeria should deliberately and proactively equip standard laboratories, train healthcare workers including epidemiologist and set up standing committees to scan the environment for challenges and curtail them. For instance, government should empower the committee to implement Strategies 1 – 11 within 14 days of any outbreak to ensure the epidemic curve is shifted to the left.

Strategy 1: Initial Baseline Assessment: This can be done in 24 hours. The committee should assess available resources (human, material, equipment, political will, policies, etc.), activities and outputs/

outcomes. What resources do we need? What resources do we have? What is the present gap? What activities have we executed? What worked well? What did not work so well? What new activities can we introduce? What activities should we stop? What activities can we modify? These analyses will give a strong background information for the next phase of the programing.

Strategy 2: Establish National and State Incident Management Teams (IMTs). National and State IMTs will include the National/State Epidemiologist, highly experienced Laboratory Manager, Communication Officer, Chief Medical Director of a tertiary facility, and a Finance Officer/manager. They should be established within 72 hours. At the Federal Level, a National IMT may comprise Director, Presidential Task Force; Director General of the national Center for Disease Control or its equivalent; Director, Emergency and Preparedness; Project Manager/ Consultant; Communication Officer and Research Lead.

Strategy 3: Capacity Development of IMTs: All national and state IMTS should be trained on the guidelines and algorithms including case definitions, epidemic thresholds, case management, infection control practices, and contact tracing. Depending on the nature of the outbreak, trainings may be virtual or physical. If highly contagious diseases like COVID-19, virtual trainings using online platforms like Zoom, Free Conference Call, GoToMeetings or other Applications to minimize physical contacts and inter-state travelling is recommended. These trainings should be facilitated by highly qualified experts from WHO, CDC, Universities and Subject Matter Experts (SMEs).

Strategy 4: Establish Testing and Diagnosis Centres: Testing and diagnosis centres with PCR capacity and right biosafety level should be established within five days in all regions or states as the case may be. Each State Governor should partner with the IMT to ensure a functional laboratory within five days. States with good capacities should establish one laboratory per Senatorial District. Every state should have at least one functional laboratory by the 10th day of the epidemic. Existing laboratories should be assessed and gaps mitigated with equipment from national reserve, stores or imported.

Strategy 5: Fund Drive: Public and private organizations, individuals and Non-governmental organizations should be encouraged to fund the entire process. Donations of money, hospitals, ambulances, consumables, laboratories, etc. should be encouraged. Governors, Senators, Honourable members, banks, oil companies, businessmen, religious groups, etc. can choose to fund one or more components of the outbreak management as they desire in one or more states.

Strategy 6: Establish Diagnosis, Isolation and Treatment (DIT) Centres. A DIT centres should be established within seven days in each state, district or region. This can be unscaled as the need arises. Self-isolation should be discouraged and people asked to be isolated in government designated locations. DITs should be located in community halls, open spaces, stadia, etc. to take the outbreak out of the hospitals. Hospitals should be free and allowed to manage the conventional illnesses and diseases common in the communities. Each DIT should have at least 200 beds and should be able to provide testing, isolation and treatment services to all suspects and confirmed cases.

Strategy 7: Human Capacity Mobilization: Government through NCDC should mobilize volunteer healthcare workers and other support staff from relevant Societies and Associations such as SPHPN, APHPN, NMA. Each group should be asked to provide at least 10 volunteers per state to work with the core team to manage the DIT centres. Where the need is more, more volunteers will be needed. Each volunteer will be trained on the management of the outbreak and their contributions will be supervised by the State IMT. Trained volunteers and healthcare workers will cascade the training downwards to others to scale up and scale out services. Volunteers will help to track contacts of confirmed cases and be engaged in community education and information management.

Strategy 8: Sample Collection Centres: Where there are no DIT centers or functional laboratories, Sample Collection Centres (SCC) will be established to collect and transfer samples to DIT centers. Simple Test Strips can be introduced for screening purposes, and those found positive will have their samples transferred to designated laboratories for confirmation and next steps.

Strategy 9: Information Management: Using internet, and other relevant platforms and applications, managers should count, divide and compare (CDC) numbers from the field and laboratory. They should use the findings to develop charts and ensure up to date information on the outbreak. This should guide evidence based decisions and polices. Also, the team should do a number of surveys using Survey Monkey, Google Forms, etc. to assess the impact of the intervention, knowledge base, attitude and practice of people.

Strategy 10: Research and Publications: Confirmed cases are vital for Randomized Control Trails. The research team should;

1. Develop a good protocol and get an expedited IRB within 14 days.

2. Experiment with different treatment combinations to identify what works best among confirmed cases.

3. Investigate patients' length of stay in hospitals

4. Investigate antigen and antibody conversion rates and factors that influence them; and

5. Investigate factors associated with various degrees of infection and manifestations, who is infected, who gets healed, who gets complicated infections, and what are the factors that influence disease outcome.

Findings should be published to advance knowledge and minimize the impact of the outbreak.

Strategy 11: Monitoring and Evaluation: There should be;

1. Daily virtual meetings at a time convenient for all to assess progress and make relevant course corrections

2. Weekly meetings to generate new ideas and review activities while giving new assignments.

3. Weekly publications on activities, finances, and lessons learned; and

4. Weekly monitoring and evaluation activities and analysis

With active use of everyday data gathered during the process of the outbreak investigation, the clinical presentation and epidemiology of the disease can be readily characterized including the use of data science, projections/modelling and data visualization.

Pulse and Reflect
Nigeria Tried to kill His Dreams but
Thankfully Canada Gave Him a Chance:

As I was finalizing this work, I saw this in on the Social Media:

''In 2014, I and several other Nigerian University graduates had been shortlisted to write the Presidential Special Scholarship (PRESSID) designed exclusively for First Class Nigerian graduates who wanted to pursue both Masters and PhD in any top 25 Universities in the world. President Goodluck Jonathan had set the scheme up and the idea was to build a strong team of brilliant Nigerians who will come back to serve the country years later. There were a little above one thousand of us who wrote the exam at CHAMS, Abuja. At the time, I was already lecturing in University of Nigeria (UNN) so most of my friends (who were also my colleagues) enrolled. 16 of us in total. It was a computer-based test so we knew our fate instantly. I had scored 94% in the exam. In fact, 15 of us from UNN scored between 80 and 97%. Man!

We came out of the exam hall completely joyous. We were so sure we had got the scholarship. And we were right. Sometime in February 2015, the list of 101 successful candidates was shortlisted in the National Dailies. Fifteen of us were on that list. I had applied to Princeton University, Imperial College London and University of Toronto already. That phase of our lives was glorious.

Fast forward to March 2015, Goodluck lost the elections to Mr. Buhari. That was where things started to take a new turn. Shortly after Mr Buhari was sworn in, he had recalled the list and complained that there was no single northerner on it.

He believed it was an agenda of the South. Right before our eyes, meritocracy was short-changed for Federal character. It was first like a joke, but we all lost that huge scholarship. It was worth about $250,000 per person (tuition and living expenses inclusive across 5 years).

Before then I had little faith in the country but when this happened, I became weary of the country.

Thankfully, later that year, I got a full scholarship from University of Toronto for my Masters and PhD (6 years in total). Of those other 14 friends of mine, 13 of them have also moved since then - US, Canada, UK, New Zealand, Japan etc.

Obviously we moved on but truth is, the life we have now was afforded to us by the Government of another country, many of which will seduce you with permanent residency and citizenship afterwards.

Any nation that short-changes merit for anything else will fall. Nigeria has the brightest people, yet, we are where we are (in Osibanjo's voice).

These people will corroborate my story as they were also winners of the PRESSID scholarship: Odoeze Jideofor Okagu Ogadimma Olikagu Sylvia Chisom Hyacinth Ali David Chukwuma Izuogu Samuel Olisa Chima Eke and others.

Sad!"

- Chidozie Ojobor'

https://www.utoronto.ca/news/u-t-phd-student-wins-global-scholarship-combating-antibiotic-resistant-superbugs

This is why RESTRUCTURING is IMPORTANT. This is why we need UNON.

The Final Word

Nigeria can bounce back to be a nation to be envied. Recently, with the recession in South Africa, Nigeria became again the largest economy in Africa. But this was not due to growing economy, but dwindling South African's economy. We need to do the right things in Nigeria.

We must bury our personal ambitions, greed, pride and decoys, to allow the nation to be rebuilt.

We must see the key challenges mentioned above and those identified by the survey as key hindrances to national growth and work assiduously to resolve them. For instance, we may not be able to do anything about the amalgamation, but we can make the best of it through Restructure and Reviewed Constitution, instalment of good and visionary leadership and administration, and citizens' education and reorientation.

Nigerians are tired of insecurity of life and property, lack of value for the lives of Nigerians, corruption (especially oil and forex), bad leaders, the effects of ethnicity/tribalism, and religiosity. These have sowed seeds of mis/distrust, discord and national disunity. We need to put these where they belong, rebuild Nigeria through better citizens' favourable policies and constitution, engage citizens productively, and establish United Nations of Nigeria.

We have lost precious time in the past 60 years. It is time to rework Nigeria by rewording the constitution and our various relationships as independent or co-dependent nationalities. We cannot continue to lie to ourselves or live in denials. It is time to be bold enough to do what is needed for a new and rebranded Nigeria.

The true change starts with you and I. Let us work to save Nigeria for the generation yet unborn.

Appendix 1

Problems and Challenges

Question: What do you think are the 3 key problems or challenges in Nigeria as a nation?

S/No	Problems or Challenges facing Nigeria as a Nation	Frequency
1	Corruption	37
2	Insecurity (including Terrorism, Insurgence)	36
3	Poor Leadership and bad administration (including bad, corrupt, unethical)	33
4	Tribalism and Ethnicity (including tribal sentiments, nepotism, discrimination, diverse ethnicity)	25
5	Religious intolerance, religiosity	21
6	Ignorance (including Poor education, educational system, aimless curriculum)	21
7	Unemployment	16

8	Poverty (including hunger, food scarcity)	11
9	Selfishness/Greed	11
10	Politics (including useless politicians	10
11	Weak Institutions and poor infrastructures	10
12	Poor accountability and mismanagement/governance of resources	9
13	Structure of Nigeria (including Quota system, monthly Federal allocation)	8
14	Poor or dehumanized Followership	7
15	Impunity/Unpatriotic	7
16	Weak Economy	6
17	Poor Electricity	5
18	Poor Health Care System	4
19	Lack of rule of Law	3
20	No Ethics/Values (including no standards)	2
21	Corrupt and non-independent Judiciary	2
22	Wrong Mind set	2
23	Indiscipline	2
24	Reward System	1
25	*Parochiasm* and Favouritism	1
26	Mediocrity	1
27	Lack of Vision	1
28	No citizens right	1
29	Ungodliness	1

30	Money	1
31	Population Explosion	1
32	Too much power in the Center	1
33	Inadequate Information Technology	1
34	Environmental problems including pollution	1
35	Crime	1
36	Military Constitution	1
		301

Appendix 2

Root Causes

Question: What do you think are the three (3) root cause(s) of these problems?

S/No	Root Causes	Frequency
1	Bad/Poor leadership and administration	40
2	Greed and Selfishness (including covetousness, self-interest)	40
3	Corruption	31
4	Ignorance and Illiteracy	22
5	Religious fanaticism (including Islamic agenda, Religious bigotry, bad teaching from religious leaders, terrorism in the name of religion	21
6	Ethnicity/Tribalism (including nepotism)	19
7	Poor Educational Practices	19
8	Politics (including lack of political will, dirty politicking, love for power)	18
9	Poverty	12

10	Failed Systems including Judiciary, electoral System	12
11	Mediocratic System	5
12	Poor Followership (including indifferent attitude, mind-set, citizens not valued)	5
13	Derailed/wrong Value Systems	5
14	Unsecure Future (including poor vision, lack of positive changes, lack of foresight)	5
15	Lack of Accountability (including misappropriation)	4
16	Mind-set (including wrong ideology, wrong doctrines, wrong priorities)	4
17	Unemployment	3
18	Traditional Practices	3
19	Colonisation, colonial legacy and dependence on the West	3
20	Disunity and mutual distrust (including incompatibility)	3
21	Lack of Value for life	3
22	Fear of domination	2
23	Pride and Ego	2
24	God Fatherism	2
25	Poor unprofessional security solving techniques	2
26	Impatience (including get rich quick)	2
27	Lack of Self Discipline	1
28	Moral Decadence	1
29	No role Models	1
30	Indiscipline	1
31	Hopelessness for Nigeria	1

32	Regionalism	1
33	Resource Zoning	1
34	Inequity	1
35	Lack of Adequate Constitution	1
36	No Public Private Partnership	1
37	Environmental Issues	1
38	Brain Drain	1
		304

Appendix 3

Perpetuating Factors

"What do you think are the three (3) main perpetuating factors sustaining these problems and challenges?

S/No	Perpetuating factors	Frequency
1	Bad Administration and Leadership (including no vision, repetition of same old leaders, no plans for citizens)	32
2	Illiteracy (including lack of proper education, poor educational system)	25
3	Greed and Selfishness	24
4	Ethnicity and Tribalism (with Nepotism)	22
5	Religious intolerance (including lack of fear of God, Muslim imposition of Sharia laws)	22
6	Corruption	20
7	Poverty (including hunger)	17

8	Mind set (including sycophancy, insincerity, ego and pride, hypocrisy, hate and dual ideology)	15
9	Failed Judiciary (including injustice of the law, lack of proper legal frameworks, selective justice, incompetence legal system, lack of justice for perpetrators, no consequence for bad or good behaviour)	15
10	Politics of bitterness (including gang up of politicians, lack of political will, politics without ideology)	13
11	Poor Accountability (including dishonesty, insincerity of government, excess money)	9
12	Poor citizens (including lack of challenges from masses, lack of awareness of masses	9
13	Inequality and inequity (including imbalance remuneration system, revenue sharing as against resource control)	7
14	Government Bureaucracy and structure (including concentration of power in the center, majority rule, states and LGA depends on Federal government)	7
15	Laziness (including people don't want to work hard any more, irresponsibility)	5

16	Lack of Patriotism	5
17	Unemployment	5
18	Insecurity	5
19	Lack of industries and electricity (including failed institutions, no infrastructures)	5
20	Government Support for evils	4
21	God Fatherism	4
22	Love for Chaos (as people in power are benefiting from the problems)	3
23	Bad role models	3
24	Dysfunctional Systems	3
25	Misplaced Priorities (with wrong choices)	3
26	Disrespect of people's culture	3
27	Love for quick money	2
28	Foreign motivators and collaborators	2
29	Dwindling economy	2
30	Deterioration of value systems	2
31	Environmental issues (including pollution)	2
32	Underdevelopment	1
33	Impunity as the corrupt are not punished	1
34	Intolerance	1
35	Lack of value for human lives	1
36	Defective constitution	1
37	Poor electoral system	1

38	Poor retirement system	1
39	Lack of meritocracy	1
40	Crude Oil reserve	1
		304

Appendix 4

Solutions and Strategies

Question: What do you think are the three (3) best possible solutions for Nigeria out of these problems?

S/No	Solutions	Frequency
1	Restructure and Review Constitution (including national split, regional autonomy, regional government, Biafra, referendum)	51
2	Good leadership/Government (including remove all in power now, visionary leadership, inclusive government, educated leadership, integrity in leadership, transfer leadership to younger generation, remove military from leadership, remove the old)	44

3	Citizens education and enlightenment (including re-orientation, love, character/ attitudinal change, moral education, remove federal character)	28
4	Free and Compulsory Education (including quality education, prioritize education, strengthen educational system, revamp and upgrade public schools)	26
5	Justice (including good and working judiciary system, social justice, stable judiciary, trusted judiciary, review policies, death punishment for looters and corrupt leaders)	15
6	Improve Security (including change security architecture, end Boko Haram, provide good welfare package for security personnel, community policing, regional/state security)	14
7	Good citizenship and followership (including accept responsibility, create awareness, change attitude, value and ethical reorientation, commitment for a new Nigeria, empowered masses)	13
8	Provide Job Opportunities (including industrialisation, public private partnerships, job security)	11

9	Overhaul Democratic Institution (including electronic voting, amend electoral laws)	10
10	Merit based System (including uphold right values)	8
11	Deemphasize money in election and make positions financially unattractive (including unattractive pay package for political office holders, reduce cost of governance)	8
12	Improve infrastructures (including electricity, ICT, basic amenities)	8
13	Political Stability (with Good political will, elect selfless leaders, hold people responsible, brand new politicians, reduce number in Senate and House of Representative)	7
14	Accountability (including right policies, checks and balances, transparency)	7
15	True Federalism (including independence of 3 arms of government)	6
16	Equity and equality for all (including effective resource management, equal opportunities)	6
17	Eliminate religious differences (including good and sincere teaching)	5

18	Patriotism mind-set and hard work	5
19	Strong systems and institutions including ICPC, EFCC, Health and education,)	4
20	The fear of God (including repent from sin, return to God)	4
21	Revolution (including mind-set revolution)	4
22	Proper resource management	4
23	End Greed and ensure contentment	3
24	Reward system (including review remuneration, improve retirement system)	3
25	Provide Enabling/learning environment	2
26	Nationalism and Unity	2
27	Recolonization and international community support	2
28	Value Humanity	2
29	End corruption	2
30	Stop Fanaticism	1
31	Enforcement of existing laws	1
32	Strategic planning	1
33	Eliminate tribalism	1
34	Improve work ethics	1
35	Contentment	1
36	Military takeover to sanitize the system	1

37	Good learning environment	1
38	War	1
39	Improve healthcare financing	1
		314

Appendix 5

Focus Solutions Areas

Question: Which problem should Nigerian Government focus as a priority?

S/No	Single Area of FOCUS	Frequency
1	Insecurity including Terrorism and religious	32
2	Fight Corruption (including money Laundry,	15
3	Restructuring and constitutional/ judiciary review	13
4	Leadership, Good and sincere government	11
5	Unemployment	10
6	Education and Health	9
7	Infrastructural Development especially Power Sector, Technology	5
8	Economy	4
9	Meritocracy	3
10	Poverty	3

11	Adherence to Rule of Law	2
12	Electoral Review	2
13	Welfare of citizens	2
14	Development in all sectors	2
15	Equity and Fairness	2
16	Create workable systems	2
17	Generational Reorientation	1
18	Education	1
19	Unethical Values	1
20	Strong institutions	1
21	Remunerations	1
22	Accountability	1
		123

Printed in the United States
By Bookmasters